DATE DUE

WORLD REVOLUTION
AND THE U.S.S.R.

THE MACMILLAN COMPANY
NEW YORK · BOSTON · CHICAGO · DALLAS
ATLANTA · SAN FRANCISCO

MACMILLAN & CO., Limited
LONDON · BOMBAY · CALCUTTA
MELBOURNE

THE MACMILLAN COMPANY
OF CANADA, Limited
TORONTO

WORLD REVOLUTION AND THE U. S. S. R.

BY

MICHAEL T. FLORINSKY, Ph.D.

ASSOCIATE IN ECONOMICS
COLUMBIA UNIVERSITY

NEW YORK
THE MACMILLAN COMPANY
1933

TO

JAMES T. SHOTWELL

PREFACE

A NEW book on Soviet Russia may need a word of explanation. Most authors writing on the U. S. S. R. put due emphasis on the fact that the former Russian Empire is governed to-day by a communist dictatorship, but, to the best of my knowledge, none of them have attempted to give even a more or less complete and comprehensive survey of the extremely important changes which have taken place in the ideas of the Russian Communist Party and of the Third International. This neglect, I think, is due to the perfectly legitimate desire to concentrate on the actual achievements of the Soviet rule and to meet the pressing demand of the reading public for authoritative and up-to-date information that will make clear how the great socialist experiment is being carried out, and to what degree it is successful. To give an answer to this would in itself be an immense and absorbing task; and it seems perfectly natural that a presumably more academic investigation of the great movement of ideas which has taken place in communist circles since 1918 and which amounts to a fundamental revision of the teachings of Marx and Lenin should, so far, have attracted little attention. A moment's reflection, however, will suggest that this movement of ideas is really a coefficient of overwhelming importance not only from the point of view of the domestic problems which the Soviet Union has to face, but also from that of the U. S. S. R. when considered as a factor in international politics.

The Soviet Union is a country of proletarian dictatorship which, again, is controlled by the Communist Party. The doctrines of the Communist Party, therefore, are of paramount importance if we are to follow intelligently the very remarkable changes which have taken place in both the domestic and the foreign policy of the Soviet Union. I do not wish to imply for a moment that the Moscow Government has been guided in its activities by purely doctrinaire considerations. On the contrary, as I am attempting to show in this small book, communist theory has, very largely, been revised under the pressure of external forces. It is only by putting the teachings of Marx, Lenin and Stalin side by side—for Stalin has been much in the picture since 1924—and by so examining their ideas, along with the interplay of political and economic considerations, that a comprehensive view of the entire situation can be obtained. I have chosen as my subject what I consider to be, and rightly so, I think, the most significant doctrine of communist theory, that of world revolution. To this subject I have tried to limit myself. It offers a key to all the economic planning and industrialization which is being carried on to-day in the Soviet Union and

to the unmistakable and fundamental change which
has taken place in the attitude of the U. S. S. R.
toward the capitalist world.

The present volume, therefore, is not a comprehensive study of the whole field of communist theory, nor is it an attempt to make a survey of the
entire field of Soviet foreign relations. Both theory
and practical politics are considered in it only in
their relation to the question of world revolution.
I have also made no attempt to describe the conflicts
and cleavages which have taken place within the
Russian Communist Party, except in so far as they
have an immediate bearing on my subject. In spite,
then, of the relatively limited scope of the present
volume I hope that it may be of some use to those
students of Russia who are interested in the less
spectacular, but nevertheless deep and fundamental
aspects of the Soviet experiment.

The two cardinal points of my discussion—Trotsky's "permanent revolution" and Stalin's "socialism in a single country"—have been dealt with by
Leon Trotsky in his book on *Permanent Revolution* and his *L'internationale communiste après
Lénine,* to which I refer in the text, and in two ap-
pendices to the third volume of his *History of the
Russian Revolution* which appeared when this present monograph was practically completed. I need
hardly say that Trotsky's statement is of great interest and historical value. His approach, however,
and the ground he has covered in his writings just
referred to, are entirely different from my own.

The sources I have gone to are, exclusively, official Soviet publications, except for books such as those of Trotsky, which, for obvious reasons, are not available in Soviet editions. I have drawn most largely from the writings of Lenin and the minutes and proceedings of various Soviet and communist bodies, particularly the congresses and conferences of the Russian Communist Party and the Third International.

For the interest taken in my work and for generous assistance, I am deeply indebted to the Social Science Research Council and the Director of its Program of Research in International Relations, Professor James T. Shotwell. They made it possible for me to visit, in 1931 and 1932, the libraries and scientific institutions of London, Paris, Geneva, Prague, Breslau and Berlin. Without these visits I could not have written the present book. The excellent libraries of Russian Historical Archives in Prague, of the Osteuropa-Institut in Breslau and of the International Labor Office in Geneva were of especial value to me in my work. The administrations of all these institutions extended to me courtesies which I feel it a privilege to be able gratefully to acknowledge here.

Professor James T. Shotwell and Professor Vladimir G. Simkhovitch have read my manuscript before publication, and I am indebted to them for many useful criticisms. They are, of course, in no way responsible for the views I have expressed.

A brief and preliminary outline of this study appeared in the *Political Science Quarterly* for June, 1932. I must thank its editor, Professor Parker T. Moon, for permission to use such material again.

I must also express my profound gratitude to Mr. Arthur E. MacFarlane for his unsparing and gallant effort to make my English less doubtful than it originally was. He is not to be blamed for imperfections which may still remain.

MICHAEL T. FLORINSKY

June 1, 1933,

Columbia University, New York.

CONTENTS

V. INTERNATIONAL IMPLICATIONS OF THE NEW DOCTRINE

VI. TOWARD COÖPERATION

WORLD REVOLUTION
AND THE U.S.S.R.

CHAPTER I

THE DOCTRINE OF WORLD REVOLUTION

THE PROBLEM

THE Union of Socialist Soviet Republics, emerging in the midst of the great war from the ruins of the Empire of the Tsars, has raised a host of new political, economic, and social problems. Among them none is perhaps more important to the capitalist world than the one that is still little known outside the Russian frontiers, the remarkable change which took place in the attitude of the Russian Communist Party and the Soviet leaders towards the question of world revolution. It has largely determined both the domestic and the foreign policy of the Soviet Union and offers the key to a number of recent developments which otherwise would appear puzzling.

It is a fact of common knowledge that the ultimate aim of communism is the establishment of a classless society which will abolish forever the exploitation of man by man, and will put into practice the chief article of faith of the communist creed, "From each according to his abilities, to each according to his needs." This great purpose is to be achieved through the overthrow of the capitalist system, which is based on the exploitation of the working classes by the capitalists, and which bears in itself

1

the germs of its own destruction. In accordance with communist teaching, the whole history of the human race is told in terms of class struggle, of a struggle between the exploiters and the exploited. This struggle naturally leads to revolutions; and the revolutions will merge in a world revolution which, via the transition period of socialism and the dictatorship of the proletariat, will lead mankind to the millennium.

But if world revolution and the ensuing breakdown of the capitalist world are both imminent and desirable, how are we to explain the present policy of the Soviet Government, which is founded upon peaceful coöperation with the capitalist countries? The first and second Five-Year Plans, as everybody knows, are based on the importation of large quantities of foreign machinery and the employment of many foreign experts and technical advisers. And the expenses involved are largely to be met from the proceeds of Soviet exports. Indeed, during the preceding years, the development of international trade relations had been one of Moscow's chief concerns. Are these activities compatible with communism's avowed intention to promote and advance world revolution by any available means? How is it possible to establish a socialist state in the Soviet Union with the assistance of the capitalist nations and at the same time destroy these very nations, essential for the realization of the most cherished communist dream? Is not coöperation with capitalist countries treason to the cause of communism?

The answer to these questions is that the attitude of the Russian Communist Party, and of the Soviet Government which it controls, towards the question of world revolution is very different in 1933 from what it was in the years immediately following the *coup d'état* of October–November, 1917. The venerable teaching of Marx and Engels went through a process of revision which continued for years and from which it emerged rejuvenated in the official program adopted by the sixth congress of the Communist International in 1928. The process itself was by no means an easy one. It took the form of a bitter struggle within the ranks of the Communist Party; and while Stalin and his followers won a decisive victory, it was purchased at the price of the ejection from the Party of some of its most prominent leaders. In this struggle the doctrine of world revolution played an extremely important part. It is hoped therefore that an outline of its evolution in the course of the fifteen years which have elapsed since the establishment of Bolshevik rule may prove useful as offering a clearer picture of the general ideas underlying the policies of the government of the U. S. S. R. and of the Third International.

THE "RELIGION" OF COMMUNISM

The bewildering spectacle of Holy Russia suddenly embracing the materialistic teaching of Marx and the missionary zeal which undoubtedly animates many of the disciples of Lenin has led numerous authors writing on Soviet conditions to describe communism as a new religion. This statement, like so many other broad generalizations, may be either true or misleading: all depends on the exact meaning which we choose to give to the word religion. The assertion itself is usually based on the rather unwarranted assumption that, hitherto, the Russian people have always been devout adherents of the Greek Orthodox Church. It seems extremely doubtful whether this statement could be adequately proved, and the remarkable ease with which the Soviet Government succeeded in stamping out religious practices within the borders of the U. S. S. R. would suggest the necessity of greater caution than is displayed by most writers when pronouncing upon the religious feelings of both Russia's peasantry and Russia's educated classes.

If we use religion in the ordinary sense of the term, meaning "human recognition of superhuman controlling power, and especially of a personal God entitled to obedience and the effect of such recognition on conduct and mental attitude," to quote the definition of the Oxford Dictionary, it will appear at once that the comparison is not valid. The communist teaching is primarily a materialistic doctrine from which any idea of superhuman control or, much more, of a personal God is rigidly excluded and, indeed, branded as vulgar superstition. The sphere of action of communism ends where the real sphere of religion begins: at that mysterious but inevitable boundary which every human being has to cross, that line which separates our earthly existence from what is beyond. Communism can win the sincere and whole-hearted support of multitudes by promising them a better existence, one from which the inequality, misery, unhappiness, and debasement which we find everywhere in the capitalist world will be eliminated. But it can do nothing to meet that irresistible urge which has it in its power to bring men and women willingly to abandon the comforts, satisfactions, and joys of this world in order to achieve what they believe to be eternal salvation. The materialistic doctrine of Marx and Lenin and the teaching of the churches appeal therefore to entirely different human emotions; and in this deeper and more fundamental aspect the two have nothing in common.

Viewed, however, from a different angle and in its more superficial aspects the comparison of communism with religion is both justifiable and useful. Like most intellectual movements with a broad social appeal, especially movements controlled by small but well-organized groups with large means at their disposal, the Russian Communist Party has been eminently successful in spreading its teaching and inspiring at least some of its followers with a missionary zeal which compares not unfavorably with that of the early Christians. It displayed a militant spirit and an intolerance towards all who did not share its gospel which will compare with the most outstanding examples offered by religious struggles. It chastised the heretics in its ranks with a ruthless savagery which may be likened, without

fear of exaggeration, to that of the Roman Inquisition, although here again the ultimate motives
are very different: In disposing of the undesirable
and erring members of the Party, communists are
concerned with the advancement of their purely
secular purposes, while the ultimate aim of the Inquisition was the salvation of the souls of the very
men and women they sent to the stake. Like the
monastic orders, the Russian Communist Party seeks
to impose upon its members a severe discipline with
a view to controlling not only their behavior but also
their way of thinking. In all these respects, no
doubt, communism and religion have a great deal in
common. But this would be largely true of any
popular social movement, as, for instance, to take
a familiar example, that of prohibition in the
United States.

There is, however, one aspect of the present situation in the Soviet Union which seems to indicate a
particularly close kinship between communism and
religion. This is the truly religious cult which has
grown up, and which now enshrines the memory and
the work of Lenin, the great leader of the Bolshevik
revolution. It would be dangerous to draw definite
conclusions from those long lines of people who wait
for hours to file by his tomb in the Red Square.
There is no way of determining whether the motives
of these communist pilgrims are similar to those of
the Russian peasants of pre-revolutionary days who
journeyed hundreds of miles to visit a holy icon in
an ancient monastery, or whether the psychology in-

volved is more like that of some contemporary crowd in New York or London which maintains a long vigil and endures great discomfort to obtain a glimpse of Charlie Chaplin, Greta Garbo, or some heavyweight champion of the world. One must remember that there are no movie stars in the U. S. S. R., and that the life of the ordinary Soviet citizen is very drab.

But if the popular attitude towards the memory of Lenin and its outward manifestations are open to more than one interpretation, there can be no question as to the supreme authority with which his writings have been clothed by the intellectual leaders of the communist movement. Strange as this may appear to anyone who is at all familiar with the Marxian dialectics, the great controversy over the question of world revolution, like all other discussions in the Soviet Union, turns largely on the interpretation of the pronouncements of the Master. The speeches and writings of the Soviet leaders bristle with quotations from Lenin. Every scrap of his work is collected, studied, annotated, and published with a zeal truly religious by a staff of learned experts of the Lenin Institute in Leningrad. The whole spirit as well as the external form of the discussion is clearly theological; and it is imbued with that intolerance and bitterness which is characteristic of disputes over religious dogmas. The proof of something is the fact that Lenin held that particular view. To be convicted of misrepresenting his opinions is to be convicted of heresy with all its inescapable consequences. It is never suggested in a communist discussion that Lenin might have made a mistake, or failed to foresee some future development. His writings are the source of all inspiration; they supply the only reliable guidance in any new political situation. He supersedes Marx and Engels as the prophet of the modern world and of the world to come. He is the sole and only Fountain of Truth.

THE DIALECTIC METHOD

It seems extremely doubtful whether this method of procedure and the use to which Lenin's writings are put by the Soviet leaders is compatible with Marxian dialectics, which are claimed to be the great and irresistible weapon of communism. The dialectic method which is traditionally associated with the name of Hegel was used with certain important modifications by Marx and Engels; and both were careful to point out that although they retained much of Hegel's logical methods and even of his peculiar terminology,[1] they were approaching the problem of historical development in a spirit which had really nothing to do with that of the German philosopher. Leaving entirely outside our discussion this involved but interesting controversy over Hegelian and Marxian dialectics, it may be useful for our purposes to obtain some idea of Lenin's attitude towards the dialectic method. A very full discussion of this all-important problem will be found in a lengthy article written by him in 1894, *Who are*

[1] The thesis, antithesis, and synthesis of the Hegelian triads.

the "Friends of the People" and how do they combat the Social-Democrats? [2] Copies of it were made on a hectograph and while most of them have since disappeared, the article was later reprinted by the Soviet Government.

"By the dialectic method," he writes, ". . . Marx and Engels understood nothing other than a scientific method in sociology which consists in considering society as a living, continuously developing organism (not as a mere mechanical conglomeration permitting arbitrary combinations of its component elements) which must be studied by an objective analysis of the conditions of production responsible for any given social formation, and by an investigation of the laws of its functioning and development." [3] Anyone who has carefully read the works of Marx and Engels cannot fail to realize, in the opinion of Lenin, that the Hegelian terminology had really nothing to do with their method, for it was concerned with "social evolution as an organic historical process of the development of social and economic formations." Lenin reminds his readers that the Marxian dialectics were not properly understood by most of his German critics after the publication of the first (German) edition of *Capital* and that its author was generally accused of "Hegelian sophistry." To refute this accusation, Marx appended to the second edition "concluding remarks"

[2] N. Lenin, *Cho takoe "druzya naroda" i kak oni voyuyut protiv sotsial-demokratov,* in *Sabranie sochineni (Collected Works),* First Edition, Vol. 1.
[3] *Ibid.,* p. 93.

in which he quotes a description of his method, as given, ominously enough, by a Russian writer.[4] This description, according to Marx, was scrupulously correct; and, following the example of Lenin, we shall here quote it in full.

"To Marx one thing is important," says the Russian; "namely, to discover the law governing the phenomena he examines, the development of these phenomena, their transition from one form into another, from one stage of social relationships into another. Marx's chief preoccupation is to show by an exact scientific investigation the necessity of given conditions of social relationships stating with all possible fullness the facts which he uses as his point of departure and on which he relies. For this purpose it is quite sufficient if, proving the necessity of the existing form of [economic and social] relations, he proves at the same time the necessity of another form of such relations which must unavoidably grow out of the one before it, irrespective of whether men believe it or not, whether they are conscious of it or not. Marx considers social development as an organic historical process controlled by laws not only independent of the will, the consciousness, and the intentions of men, but on the contrary laws that determine their will, consciousness, and intentions. . . . If the element of consciousness plays so subordinate a part in the history of culture, it will be readily understood that criticism, directed against this culture itself, cannot be very well based on any

[4] In *Vestnik Evropi (European Messenger)*, No. 5, 1872.

form or any result of consciousness. In other words, its point of departure must be certainly not an idea, but only an external, objective phenomenon. Criticism must consist in comparing a given fact not with an idea, but with another fact; the only important condition is that both facts should be carefully investigated and that they should represent, in their mutual relationship, different moments of development, and it is particularly important that the same careful investigation should be applied to the whole series of known stages, their sequence, and the interdependence of their various stages of development. Marx specifically denies the theory that economic laws are the same for the past and for the present. On the contrary, each historical period has its own laws. Economic development presents a phenomenon analogous to the history of other fields of biology. The early economists did not understand the nature of the economic laws when they compared them with the laws of physics and chemistry. A more careful analysis has made it plain that social organisms differ among themselves as much as the organisms of plants and animals. By determining his problem as the investigation of the economic organization of capitalism from this point of view, Marx had given at the same time a strictly scientific formulation of the aims which must be pursued in every investigation of economic developments. The scientific significance of such an investigation consists in bringing out these special (historical) laws which regulate the appearance, existence, development, and death of a given organism and its replacement by another and higher organism." [5]

After quoting this description of the dialectic method as the best account of it that had ever come to his attention, Marx states that his method is really "the inverse" of the method of Hegel. In accordance with Hegel, the development of the idea determines the actual development. But Marx, on the contrary, teaches that "the ideal is merely a reflection of the material," and that the whole process is therefore reduced to "the positive understanding of the present and of its necessary development."

Such is, in brief, the authoritative statement of the nature of the dialectic method endorsed by both Marx and Lenin. It is claimed by the socialists that it has put in their hands a weapon of irresistible power and an instrument of unerring precision which permits not only a trustworthy and comprehensive analysis of the past and of the present, but also an unfailing forecast of the future. Whatever we may think of these claims, it will be readily understood that the successful application of the dialectic method to any particular problem is by no means an easy task. An illuminating illustration of Lenin's own opinion of his colleagues' skill in Marxian dialectics is given in the last letter written by him before his death, one written to the Executive Committee of the Union and usually known as his testament. Discussing the qualifications of Nicholas Bukharin, until quite recently one of the outstand-

[5] Lenin, *op. cit.*, pp. 93–95.

ing figures of the Bolshevik Olympus and one of the most authoritative writers on communist theory, Lenin writes: "Bukharin is not only the most valuable and the most important dialectician of the Party, but also is deservedly looked upon as the favorite of the entire Party; nevertheless his theoretical views can hardly be accepted as truly Marxian because there is something scholastic about him. He was never trained in dialectics and, I think, never fully understood them."[6] How a man who was never trained in the dialectic method and never fully understood it could in spite of this be the Party's "most valuable and important dialectician" is perhaps as difficult to comprehend as the application of the dialectic method itself. But it seems reasonably certain that Lenin, if he could come back, would not hesitate to brand as un-Marxian and scholastic the discussions carried on since his death by his disciples, discussions in which his name and writings play so important a part, just as he would probably condemn as a gross and vulgar superstition the homage paid to his tomb by multitudes of semiliterate Russian peasants.

There is another characteristic feature of the communist procedure which we will meet over and over again in the course of our investigation. This is the outstanding place given in their discussions to fu-

---

[6] J. Stalin, *O pravom uklone v VKP (On the Right Opposition in the Communist Bolshevik Party)*, p. 63, quoted in M. Gaisinsky, *Borba s uklonami ot generalnoi linii Partii (Struggle Against the Deviations from the General Line of the Party)*, Moscow-Leningrad, 1930, p. 177.

ture events. Marxian dialectics, as we have pointed out, are supposed to provide unfailing rules for forecasting developments to come. With reference to the fate of the capitalistic system with which Marx and Lenin are chiefly concerned, they have reached the conclusion that it is doomed to disappear "irrespective of whether men believe it or not, or whether they are conscious of it or not." The followers of Lenin believe in the impending collapse of capitalism and are fully conscious of it; and this has made them talk about the future, and, what is still worse, about the near future, with an assurance and a degree of precision which later they have had reasons to regret. The use of the future tense in political discussions has both advantages and disadvantages. It offers an easy escape from the often unattractive conditions of the present and allows one to forget the disappointments and hardships of to-day by evoking the radiant images of better days to come, especially when these better days are, assuredly, almost within one's reach, or just around the corner. The baffling of these hopes and the nonfulfilment of these promises are the reverse of the medal, as communist leaders have gradually learnt from their experiences in 1918–1920 as well as on many other occasions.

LENIN AND WORLD REVOLUTION

In view of the decisive importance attached to-day by the communists to the opinions of Lenin, it may be useful to obtain at this stage some idea of his attitude with respect to the immediate prospect of a world revolution. His writings, to repeat, will be frequently quoted by the partisans of the opposing factions. There is evidence that he was not immune from the excessive revolutionary enthusiasm which swept his followers in the early days of the revolution. Nevertheless he sounded a note of caution against exuberant hopes, and sounded it with a consistency which few of the Bolshevik leaders can boast of.

"The proletarian flag of civil war," he wrote in 1914, "will gather around it—if not to-day, then to-morrow, if not during the present war, then after it, or in the war next to come—not only hundreds of thousands of responsible workers, but also millions of semi-proletarians and small bourgeois, to-day bamboozled by chauvinistic ideas. For the horror of war will not only terrify and benumb, but it will also enlighten, teach, organize, strengthen, and prepare them for a war against the bourgeoisie in their own country and in foreign countries."[7]

In an article written in 1915 and directed against Kautsky and the socialists of his school, Lenin amplified his statement. "How long will the present situation last and how much more acute will it become?" he wrote. "Will it lead to revolution? We do not know, and no one can possibly know. The answer will be given only with the growth of revolutionary feelings and when the most advanced social group, the proletariat, decides to take action.

[7] N. Lenin, Vol. XIII, p. 17.

There can be no question here of any 'illusions' and there not being fulfilled, because nowhere and at no time did a socialist ever take it upon himself to guarantee that the revolution would be brought about by *this*, and not by the next war, by the revolutionary situation of to-day, and not by that of to-morrow. We are speaking here of the most fundamental and most indisputable duty of every socialist, the duty to reveal to the masses the existence of a revolutionary situation, to explain to them its depth and possibilities, to awake the revolutionary conscience and determination of the proletariat, to assist it in taking revolutionary action, and to create an organization suitable for carrying on this work in the existing revolutionary situation." [8]

The same cautious attitude was displayed by Lenin about three weeks before the Bolshevik *coup d'état:* "I do not know whether we shall win to-morrow or a little later. Personally I am inclined to think that we shall win to-morrow—I am writing these lines on October 6, 1917—and that we may be too slow in seizing power; anyhow, to-morrow is to-morrow, and not to-day. We do not know how soon our victory will be followed by a revolution in western countries. We do not know whether our victory will not be followed by a transition period of reaction and by victory for the counter-revolution." [9]

[8] N. Lenin, Vol. XIII, p. 142.
[9] Quoted by Thälmann, see *Chetverti Vsemirni Kongress Kommunisticheskago Internatsionala (The Fourth World Congress of the Communist International),* selected reports and resolutions, Moscow-Petrograd, 1923, p. 214.

A similar element of caution as to the immediate revolutionary outlook may be detected in the pronouncements of Lenin during the discussion which took place in 1918 in connection with the Brest-Litovsk Peace. He repeated his warning at the opening of the second congress of the Communist International in 1920 when the victorious advance of the Red army towards the capital of Poland was interpreted by many of his followers as the final blow to capitalism, at least in eastern Europe.

"We have now," said Lenin, "approached the question of the revolutionary crisis as a basis of our revolutionary action, and here I must draw your attention to two widespread errors. On the one hand, the bourgeois economists represent the present crisis as an unpleasant disturbance, to use the elegant expression of some English writers. On the other, some revolutionaries attempt to prove that the crisis is absolutely without an issue. This, however, is a mistake; there is no such thing as a situation absolutely without an issue. The bourgeoisie behaves like a crazed wild beast; it piles up stupid mistakes that accelerate its own ruin. All this is true. But you cannot 'prove' that it is absolutely impossible for the bourgeoisie to quiet a certain minority of the exploited by certain small concessions, that it will not succeed in suppressing a certain uprising or movement among a certain group of the debased and exploited population. To attempt beforehand to prove that a situation is 'absolutely without issue' would be mere pedantry or a futile exercise for idle minds. Facts alone are the only real 'proofs' in this and similar questions. The bourgeois system throughout the world is passing through a severe crisis. It is necessary to 'prove' now, by the action of the revolutionary party, that it has sufficient organization and capacity to coöperate with the exploited masses, sufficient determination and skill to use the crisis to bring about a successful, victorious revolution." [10]

Karl Radek maintains, in an article written, it is true, in 1931, that Lenin had foreseen a long period of struggle between the proletariat and the capitalistic system, a period crowded with national revolutions and colonial uprisings, and that the final transformation of democratic revolutions and nationalistic uprisings in the East into the great socialist world revolution would be a slow and lengthy process. [11]

TROTSKY'S "PERMANENT REVOLUTION"

The doctrine of world revolution received its fullest and most eloquent expression under the able and prolific pen of one of Lenin's principal lieutenants in the days of October, the former commander-in-chief of the Red army and now an exile at Prinkipo, the indomitable, fiery, versatile Leon Trotsky.

Trotsky's part in the revolutionary events of 1905, 1917, and the following years is too well known

[10] N. Lenin, Vol. XVII, pp. 263–264.
[11] Karl Radek, *Leninskoe uchenie o mirovoi revolyutsii v svete istoricheskoi proverki (Lenin's Doctrine of World Revolution in the Light of Historical Developments),* in *Izvestia,* January 22, 1931.

to need to be retold here. No other Russian revolutionary leader, not even Lenin himself, has enjoyed
so wide an international audience, above all since his
enforced leisure in Turkey has permitted him to
devote the whole of his time to literary work, in
which he has displayed remarkable ability. Nor has
any excessive modesty kept him from claiming what
he considered to be—and often on excellent ground
—his due. His final break with the Soviet leaders
who gradually made their way to the controlling position in the Communist Party and the Soviet Government dates back to the autumn of 1924, when the
new formula or slogan, "Socialism in a single country," was first given forth by Stalin, and found itself in irreconcilable opposition to Trotsky's theory
of "permanent revolution." Leaving for a later
chapter the examination of this all-important controversy, whose issue largely determined the entire
course of the Soviet's coming domestic and foreign
policy as well as the policies of the Third International, we may now consider Trotsky's conception of
revolutionary development. It will probably be no
exaggeration to say that for the first six or seven
years of communist rule in Russia the theory of
"permanent revolution" in its international aspect
was a generally accepted principle of the communist
faith.

The theory itself is by no means new. It was first
formulated by Trotsky in articles dating back to the
events which preceded the revolutionary outbreak
of 1905, and was amplified and developed in his later

writings. The most complete and up-to-date statement of the theory of "permanent revolution" will be found in a little book written in 1928 at Alma-Ata, where Trotsky was forced to spend several months previous to his departure for Turkey.[12] Faithful to Marxian dialectics, Trotsky understands by permanent revolution a revolution which does not accept any forms of class domination, and does not stop at the democratic stage, but proceeds to enforce socialist policies and to wage war against reaction from the outside, a revolution "whose every successive stage is rooted in the previous one, and which can only end with the final liquidation of class society." The theory of permanent revolution embraces three separate sets of ideas: (1) the merging of a democratic revolution in a socialist revolution; (2) the gradual transformation of society itself during the period of socialist revolution; and (3) the international aspect of the socialist revolution. Each of these points needs elucidation.

The fundamental idea of permanent revolution— the necessary merging of the democratic revolution in the socialist revolution—is traced by Trotsky to

[12] Among the earlier works of Trotsky dealing with the general course of revolutionary development the most important one is the article, *Itogi i perspektivi (Past Achievements and the Outlook),* in his volume, *Nash revolyutsia,* St. Petersburg, 1906, pp. 224–286; also the Foreword written, in 1922, to his volume, *"1905."*

A comprehensive statement of Trotsky's view on the subject will be found in his *Permanentnaya revolyutsia,* Berlin, 1930. The English translation of this volume *(The Permanent Revolution,* translated by Max Shachtman, Pioneer Publishers, New York, 1931) has an interesting preface which does not appear in the Russian edition.

Marx. It was Marx who first formulated this great
principle as a reply to the contention of democratic
leaders who believed that the establishment of a "reasonable"—that is, democratic—form of government
would make possible the solution of all social and economic problems through peaceful evolution. To
Marx the bourgeois revolution of 1848 was merely the
stepping-stone to the socialist revolution. These expectations failed to materialize, but the "error" of
Marx was one of fact, not of method. The revolution
of 1848 did not lead to a democratic form of government, but to the dictatorship of the bourgeoisie. The
same is true of the German revolution of 1918, which
was a genuine proletarian revolution which failed
because of the predatory policies of its social-
democratic leaders, and ended in a bourgeois counter-
revolution camouflaged as a democratic régime. The
conventional school of so-called Marxian socialists,
both in Russia and in foreign countries, has worked
out a theory of the historical development of society
in accordance with which every society sooner or
later reaches the democratic form of organization
and then proceeds to establish socialism. The transition from democracy to socialism is variously represented. By some it is believed that it will be
achieved through a peaceful evolution. Other
branches of this school believe in the necessity of
violent revolutionary methods. The important feature, which all have in common, is this, and it applies
to all peoples and all countries: they consider democracy and socialism as two stages of historical de-

velopment which are not only quite distinct, but are also separated by lengthy periods of time. Plekhanov, Russia's eminent socialist leader, declared nonsensical the very idea that socialism was possible in contemporary Russia. And to the present leaders of the Russian Communist Party the prospect of a socialist revolution not only in 1905, but even on the very eve of the October *coup d'état,* seemed to be merely "the confused music of a distant future."

The theory of permanent revolution revived by Trotsky in 1905 was directed against this point of view. It proceeded to show that the democratic aspirations of modern backward capitalist nations must necessarily lead to the dictatorship of the proletariat and that the latter inevitably results in the enforcement of socialist policies. This, says Trotsky, is the central idea of the theory. In flagrant contradiction to the generally accepted view, democracy and socialism were declared to be not two distinct and widely separated stages of historical development but two moments in the same historical process, the former leading immediately and necessarily to the latter. The "permanency" of the revolutionary development was therefore established.

The transformation of society under the dictatorship of the proletariat forms the second important feature of the theory of permanent revolution. As class society is still in existence—this is why the dictatorship of the proletariat is to be maintained—this process of transformation will necessarily take the shape of a class struggle. It will require an undetermined and perhaps lengthy period of time and comprise periods of civil and foreign wars as well as periods of peaceful evolution. The process itself is strictly dialectic, every subsequent stage growing organically from the preceding one. It will effect revolutionary changes in all spheres of human activity, in economic organization, technique, science, family relationships, social habits. The changes, being both continuous and closely interrelated, prevent society from reaching a state of equilibrium. Thus the "permanency" of revolution is again emphasized.

The international implications of the theory of permanent revolution which are of particular interest to us in this study are the direct outcome of the present stage in the economic and political development of the human race. All the countries in the world are to-day closely interdependent. Just as every nation is producing for the world market and is intimately affected by the economic changes which take place in the remotest parts of the globe, so the class struggle of the proletariat is conducted on a world scale. It is true that a socialist revolution begins on national soil; but it cannot reach a successful conclusion—the elimination of class society—within national frontiers. The proletarian dictatorship in an isolated country is but a provisional régime, although it may be a lasting one, as has been proved by the case of the U. S. S. R. But under these conditions, antagonisms both internal and external are bound to arise and will lead the isolated proletarian state to its doom unless it is rescued by a victorious revolution in several advanced countries. From this point of view, says Trotsky, "a national revolution is not a self-contained unit; it is just a link in the international chain. The international revolution is a permanent process in spite of the temporary setbacks and the ebbing of the tide."

This scheme of revolutionary development is not merely a scholastic conception to occupy the minds of Red professors. It is, to repeat, a formulation of general principles which for a time have largely determined the policies of one of the Great Powers. Before 1924 one of the most contested parts of Trotsky's doctrine was its first contention, the necessary merging of the democratic revolution in a socialist revolution. If one shares his view that the socialist stage immediately follows the democratic, the question arises, what social group, what class is to assume the responsibility of government, to exercise the dictatorship? Lenin's formula, advanced during the Revolution of 1905, spoke of the "democratic dictatorship of the workers and peasants." This formula, Trotsky maintains, was "algebraic"; it merely stated that the exploited classes will be irreconcilably opposed to the bourgeoisie, but it refused to determine in advance their interrelationship during the period of the dictatorship. The proposed alliance of the proletariat with the peasantry in a revolutionary dictatorship was something that so far had never been known in history, and this was why Lenin intentionally gave his solution a general or abstract character. The attitude of the peasantry was the "great unknown" which made it impossible to forecast the exact course of revolutionary development. Lenin believed in those days, as he did in the years immediately following, that revolutionary developments were bound to result in the creation of a strong and well-organized peasant party. "There is not the slightest doubt," he wrote in 1909, "that a revolution which has reached . . . so advanced a stage as that of a revolutionary dictatorship, will create a better organized and a stronger revolutionary peasant party. To argue otherwise is to assume that some of the essential organs of a full-grown man remain infantile in their size, form, and degree of development." [13] The events of 1917 have proved conclusively, in the opinion of Trotsky, that the peasantry is incapable of creating such a party, and that at the critical moment it must accept the leadership of either the bourgeoisie or of the proletariat. This is why the only possible form of dictatorship for the transition period between capitalism and the classless society of the future is the "dictatorship of a proletariat which leads the masses of the peasantry." Lenin seems to have accepted this view in 1918 when he wrote: "The whole science of economics, if any lesson can be drawn from it, the whole history of the revolution, the whole history of the political development of the nineteenth century, teaches us that the peasant follows either the worker or the bourgeois. If I were asked why, I should suggest that those who ask me . . . meditate upon the develop-

[13] N. Lenin, Vol. XI, Part I, p. 230.

ment of any important revolution of the eighteenth and the nineteenth century, or the political history of any country in the twentieth century. The economics of capitalist society are such that the one dominating force must be either capital, or the proletariat that overthrows it. There is no other force in the economics of this society." [14] These remarks, Trotsky points out, refer to revolutions in backward countries—this is why Lenin uses the eighteenth and the nineteenth centuries as his example—and they completely rule out the possibility of any "democratic" dictatorship. The dictatorship of the proletariat is the only conceivable and practicable form.

The immense practical importance of this principle will be perceived at once. On the one hand, it determines the interrelationship between the two elements in the revolution, the proletariat and the peasantry; on the other, it indicates the policy which the Soviet Government and the Third International are to follow in the matter of revolutionary outbreaks in other countries, especially in the colonial and semi-colonial countries. One of the standard accusations against "Trotskyism" is that it overlooks or ignores the part which the peasantry plays in a successful revolution. These accusations seem to be devoid of foundation. Trotsky emphasized in innumerable articles and speeches the immense importance of the peasantry in any revolutionary outbreak. He stated, indeed, on more than one occasion that the whole-hearted participation of the peas-

[14] N. Lenin, Vol. XVI, p. 217.

antry in the revolutionary movement was an essential element of success. But he had also maintained that the dictatorship could not be democratic, it could not be a combination of the proletariat and the peasants, but should be entirely in the hands of the former. It was a part of the duties of a proletarian dictatorship to secure, through an enlightened policy, the collaboration of the masses of the peasants.

In the international field the rejection of the principle of proletarian dictatorship as the only possible form has led, in the opinion of Trotsky, to the complete failure of Stalin and the Third International to organize, guide, and support the revolutionary outbreaks in foreign countries, especially in the East. The most flagrant example of this failure is, in his opinion, the policies of the Moscow communists with reference to China and the ensuing collapse of the Chinese revolution.

All the elements of the doctrine of permanent revolution, its author maintains, constitute a comprehensive program of action, one determining the other. After the proletariat has seized power and established its dictatorship it proceeds to enforce socialist measures which undermine the very foundations of capitalist society. But socialist policies within national frontiers are not a goal in themselves but merely a stepping-stone towards the bringing about of revolution in at least a number of advanced industrial countries, without which no socialist society can be built up. These policies, therefore, should not aim at something that cannot be achieved—namely, the creation of socialism within one country only—but should be used in a manner that will serve the ultimate purpose of world revolution. While strengthening and consolidating its internal position, the triumphant proletariat must always keep in mind this ultimate goal which must inspire it and must dominate its handling of domestic problems and its relations with foreign countries. The sacrifice of world revolution to the requirements of establishing a national socialist state is not only a betrayal of the communist cause but also a suicidal and insane policy, which refuses to see existing conditions, the economic and political interdependence of the world, and prepares its own inevitable downfall. It is this aspect of the theory of permanent revolution which becomes the chief point of contention between Stalin and Trotsky in the autumn of 1924.

Taken as a whole, the doctrine of permanent revolution is not without logical unity and a certain grandeur. Trotsky fought stubbornly for it, and preferred to take the road of exile rather than to surrender to his enemies.

CHAPTER II

THE PERIOD OF "STURM UND DRANG," 1918–1920

THE MORROW OF OCTOBER

THE downfall of Russian tsardom in March, 1917, was followed in October (November) of the same year by the seizure of power by the Bolsheviks and the eventual establishment of the dictatorship of the proletariat. Looking back at the crowded years through which Russia has lived since the beginning of the century, it seems reasonably clear to-day that the two revolutions of 1917—the overthrow of the monarchy and the advent of the Soviets—were merely two stages of the same historical process, one fully prepared by the political, economic, and social conditions which had been growing up in the country since the days of the emancipation of the serfs in 1861.[1] But it is easy to be wise after the event. The troubled days of 1917 were hardly a suitable time for historical analysis; and what appears to us now as a logical and, indeed, necessary result of a given set of historical conditions seemed most uncertain and confused in the midst of the immense upheaval which combined all the destructive

[1] For the author's interpretation of the Russian revolution, see Michael T. Florinsky, *The End of the Russian Empire,* Yale University Press, 1931.

and creative elements of a great war, the smashing of an ancient dynasty, the destruction of a firmly rooted political system, the tidal wave of a vast peasant uprising, and a social revolution on a scale without precedent in the annals of the human race. Paradoxical as this may sound, even the abdication of the Tsar, which was generally expected and much discussed in 1916 and the early weeks of 1917, nevertheless took the country by surprise. Events immediately assumed a turn which the leaders of the old liberal opposition had not foreseen and for which they were not ready. Prince Lvov, the first head of the Provisional Government, which took office in March, 1917, frankly admitted a few weeks later that circumstances had carried him and his colleagues much farther than they had intended to go. "We are tossed about," he said, "like *débris* on a stormy sea." [2]

But if the revolution found the leaders of the Russian liberals asleep like the foolish virgins of the parable, the revolutionary socialists, who soon succeeded the Provisional Government as the rulers of the former Empire of the Tsars, were hardly better prepared. The underground revolutionary societies of pre-war days, which never enjoyed anything like the influence often ascribed to them abroad, had been almost annihilated by the Imperial Government in a campaign of repression which followed the strikes of June–July, 1914. Their activities during the war were at low ebb. Most

[2] *Ibid.*, p. 245.

of the important revolutionary leaders were either abroad or in prison. Lenin was in Switzerland and did not reach Petrograd until the beginning of April, 1917. Trotsky was in New York and came to Russia a month later. The whole work of the Bolshevik party in Petrograd, according to one of its members, Shlyapnikov, was carried on during the first two weeks after the revolution by only three men. There was practically no party machinery, no funds, no printing equipment. Even more important, perhaps, was the complete lack of agreement between revolutionary leaders. The Social-Revolutionary Party, traditionally considered as representing the peasantry, was at odds with the Social-Democratic Party which, again, was split by a deep cleavage between the Bolshevik and the Menshevik wings. Even among the Bolsheviks themselves there was little unanimity of policy. The teaching of Lenin and Trotsky that the democratic revolution of March must be immediately followed by a socialist revolution was slow in making converts, and many were those among the old party workers who still believe that a more or less protracted period of democracy was a necessary stage through which the country had to pass before it was ripe for socialism. Such views were expressed by Stalin immediately after the downfall of the Empire and a little later by Kamenev, Rykov, and Zinoviev, who tried to convince Lenin that a socialist revolution in Russia was impracticable unless it was preceded by the overthrow of capitalism in England and other advanced countries. But the great forces set loose by the revolution were working for the Bolshevik cause. The slogans Lenin had written on his banner, "An immediate end to the war," "All land for the peasants," and "Make plunder of what had been plundered" (that is, distribute all private wealth among the workers), were exactly those which represented the long-suppressed wishes of the land-hungry and war-weary peasantry. The Provisional Government of the liberals and moderate socialists gave way to the Bolsheviks in October with no more effort than they themselves had had to put forth to displace the Tsar eight months earlier. And the new rulers of the country were no less surprised than their predecessors to find themselves in control of the immense Empire and no less uncertain as to what policy to follow. Even those among the Bolsheviks who took an immediate and leading part in the events which resulted in their advent to power were most uncertain about the future. Trotsky, who with Lenin was the guiding spirit of the Bolshevik uprising of October, 1917, has frankly admitted that "it was impossible to tell in advance whether we were to stay in power or be overthrown." And many of his colleagues made no secret of their disapproval of a step that they considered rash and, indeed, suicidal.

It is only natural that amid the overpowering difficulties which the Bolsheviks encountered in the early days of their rule they should turn for relief and, perhaps, salvation to the world revolution. Few of them doubted in those days that a delay in the outbreak of a socialist revolution in at least some of the more advanced countries would result in the collapse of their own rule. But the coveted prize seemed to be well within their reach. Was not the world exhausted by the deadly convulsions of a war which had already lasted for more than three years? Were not the men in the armies of the Allies and Germany just as tired and weary as their fellow soldiers in Russia? Did not the city workers experience unexampled privations? It seemed clear that the world was about to follow the example set up by the proletariat of Russia. The triumph of the Russian revolution was the spark which could but start a world conflagration in that Europe of 1918–1919, so heavily laden with explosives. The only thing to do was to explain to the nations of the world the easy method by which Russia had rid herself not only of the Tsar but also of bourgeois exploitation. The argument was irresistible, and it was bound to bear its fruit.

This was the general attitude in Petrograd and Moscow in 1918–1920, a period of heroic struggle against the White forces supported by the Allied Powers and by the United States, a time of real revolutionary enthusiasm and missionary zeal which Zinoviev has aptly described as the period of "Sturm und Drang." [3] The communist leaders believed that the call to arms against the oppressor could not but

[3] G. Zinoviev, *Bolshevizatsya partii (The Bolshevization of the Party)*, in *Kommunisticheski Internatsional (Communist International)*, 1925, No. 1, p. 3.

awaken the revolutionary masses of the workers of
the world. They could not fail to respond when they
had been given the message. And this was to be
brought to them through the instrumentality of
both the Soviet state and the Third International.

THE BREST-LITOVSK NEGOTIATIONS

The policy of direct incitement to revolution dominated the international activities of the Soviet Government in the course of the first two or three years
of its rule. This policy, of course, was not dictated
entirely by doctrinaire considerations and was largely
a matter of expediency, a natural outgrowth of the
position of complete isolation from the outside
world in which Russia found herself, first as a result of the peace of Brest-Litovsk, and, later, of the
blockade of Russia by the Allies and the exigencies
of the civil war in which the White troops were supported by the Allied Powers. Great Britain, France,
Italy, and the smaller Allies were greatly shocked
by what had taken place in Russia and considered,
not without good reason, that the abandonment of
the cause of the Allies by the Soviet Government
was something akin to treason. To the flood of
revolutionary propaganda which came across the
Russian frontier they responded after the signing
of the armistice in November, 1918, by establishing
a *cordon sanitaire* along the western frontier of the
former Russian Empire. A wholly irrational over-
rating of the effectiveness of revolutionary propaganda is one of the outstanding characteristics of

this period. In a world deeply shaken by the war, in the midst of crumbling thrones and institutions, and of a wholesale reshuffling of frontiers which raised bitter national and social antagonisms, the Bolsheviks were not the only ones to believe that revolutionary propaganda was a most powerful, perhaps a decisive, weapon. On the other hand, in those days, few European statesmen would admit the possibility of a Soviet Government's lasting for fifteen years; that is, almost indefinitely. We have seen that the Bolsheviks themselves considered their own future to be highly uncertain. It was generally thought in European capitals that their rule would be of short duration, if only one could manage to keep the masses at home from being contaminated by the deadly poison. Bolshevik propaganda in its most direct and aggressive form was held to be the chief danger on one side of the boundary, and the chief weapon on the other.

The firm belief in the imminence of a world revolution which prevailed in important Soviet circles is well illustrated by the course of the peace negotiations of Brest-Litovsk and the discussion which arose in this connection within the Bolshevik Party. The negotiations themselves were freely used by the Soviet plenipotentiaries, headed first by Joffe and then by Trotsky, primarily as an exceptional opportunity for revolutionary propaganda among the war-weary people of Germany, Austria-Hungary, Bulgaria, and Turkey. The more cautious attitude of Lenin was confronted with the uncompromising views of the so-called Left Wing communists and of Trotsky. The Left Wing communists advocated a holy war. They considered the situation then existing in Europe as particularly favorable to the advancement of world revolution, and interpreted the strikes which were taking place in Austria and Germany as the first steps of the proletarian uprising. In their opinion, the world revolution was not only ripe, but had actually begun. They realized, of course, that Soviet Russia was anything but ready for war; but they believed that when the detachments of the Red army met the German troops they would not fight, but would join hands and wage together a holy war against the world bourgeoisie. Much was expected by the Left Wing communists from the so-called "trench peace"; that is, the fraternizing between the German soldiers in the trenches and their Russian opponents. This was, in their opinion, the only way of gaining the real objective of the communists, while a separate peace with the German imperialists would lead not to the breathing space advocated by Lenin, but would spell the doom of both the Russian and the world revolution.

Trotsky, while sharing the belief in the general principles on which the argument of the Left Wing communists was based, drew from them a somewhat different conclusion. His was the celebrated formula, "No war, no peace"; that is, to declare the war ended and the army demobilized without making any actual peace with the enemy. This policy was based on the idea that the Germans would not dare to advance into Russia. It was officially sanctioned by the Council of People's Commissars over the objections of Lenin and led to the breaking off of the negotiations. The belief of Trotsky in the immense propaganda value of his "great gesture" persisted even after the Germans proceeded to advance into Russia. He was vigorously supported by the Left communists. "We have maintained," said Bukharin, "that the Russian revolution will either expand, or will be crushed by world imperialism." And the opinion was advanced that the interests of the Russian revolution must be sacrificed to those of world revolution. The very wiping out of the Russian revolution might serve that higher purpose. "Our strangling," said Lomov, "may help to bring about the revolution in the west." On the other hand, the preservation of the Russian revolutionary government, it was argued, might prove fatal to world revolution. "By saving our socialist republic," said Bukharin, "we are losing the chance of promoting world revolution." [4]

The firm attitude of the German Government and the rapid advance of the German troops into Russian territory, and in the direction of Petrograd, forced the Soviet Government to abandon its former policy. On the receipt of the news of the occupation of Dvinsk by the Germans, the Executive Committee decided by a vote of 7 to 6 to yield unconditionally

[4] *Protokoli Tsentralnago Komiteta RSDRP (Minutes of the Central Committee of the Russian Social Democratic Workers' Party)*, xxx, published by the Lenin Institute, quoted in Gaisinsky, *op. cit.*, pp. 23–24.

to the demands of the Central Powers. And thus they discarded the earlier policy of "No war, no peace," as well as the alternative proposal for a holy war. Compliance with the demands of the Germans was advocated by Lenin from the very beginning of the negotiations as a matter of urgent necessity, and as the only method of saving Bolshevist Russia, the stronghold of revolution, from destruction. It is indicative of the general frame of mind of the Soviet leaders that this view, in spite of Lenin's authority, was originally rejected and was finally accepted only under menace of German bayonets. On February 23, 1918, the Soviet Government agreed to the crushing terms of Germany, and the Treaty of Brest-Litovsk was signed on March 3. It was believed at the time in Petrograd and Moscow (the government moved to Moscow on March 11) that the Treaty of Brest-Litovsk would prove just another scrap of paper. These expectations were not disappointed, though the annulment of the Brest-Litovsk Treaty was brought about not by a communist revolution in the Central Powers, as was anticipated in Russia, but by the military defeat of Germany. It was, indeed, provided for in the terms of the armistice of November, 1918.

The breathing space which Lenin secured for his country by his Brest-Litovsk policy has since been held to be one of his greatest achievements and a striking manifestation of his political genius. There is no doubt that on this occasion he displayed a much keener sense of political reality than many of his colleagues, who insisted upon seeing in the world revolution the only method for the solution of their immediate problems.

The signature of the Treaty of Brest-Litovsk not only saved the Soviet Government from probable destruction, but also provided it with an opportunity to proceed with an intensive campaign of revolutionary propaganda in Central Europe. The centre of these activities was the Soviet Embassy in Berlin headed by the expert revolutionary, A. A. Joffe. The Soviet Ambassador has since claimed his share of credit for the overthrow of the German Imperial Government.[5] He was so active that on November 5, 1918, he was ordered to leave Berlin with his entire staff. Diplomatic relations with Germany were not resumed until 1922.

ZINOVIEV'S ARTICLES

Except for Joffe's short-lived mission to Berlin, Soviet Russia remained practically isolated from the outside world until the end of the civil war; that is, until the autumn of 1920. But if during the whole of this period there were no direct relations between Moscow and the foreign capitals, at no time did international affairs occupy a larger place in the preoccupations of Bolshevik leaders, nor were those leaders at any time more internationally minded. This intense if somewhat one-sided interest in world affairs was determined not only by the hostile atti-

[5] *Vestnik Zhizni*, No. 5, Moscow, 1919, quoted in Louis Fisher, *The Soviets in World Affairs*, New York, 1930, Vol. I, p. 75.

tude of the capitalist powers and their reluctance to
admit that the Soviet Union had come to stay, but
also by the firm belief among the new rulers of Russia that revolution in the more advanced countries
was a thing of the very near future. This belief
was expressed with particular force in the speeches
and articles of one of the leading figures of the Russian Communist Party of that period, G. Zinoviev,
the former president of the Third (Communist) International. His name acquired wide notoriety in
connection with the so-called "Zinoviev letter,"
which played an important part in the British elections of 1924, and the authenticity of which is still
open to doubt. The vicissitudes of his later career,
and his eventual complete eclipse accompanied by
his recent expulsion from the Communist Party in
no way diminish the authority and importance of
his earlier pronouncements. To discount the value
of his statements of 1919 on the ground of his in-
ability to maintain his position in the years to
come would be just as unjustified as to deny the
part of Trotsky in the *coup d'état* of October because he was forced to go into exile in Turkey in
1928, or to measure the leadership of Mr. Lloyd
George during the war and in 1918 by the size of his
following in the Parliament of 1931.

Mr. Lloyd George is reported to have said on one
occasion that his speeches were his worst enemies.
The record of his declarations in the electoral campaign of November–December, 1918, offers ample
justification for this sad reflection. Zinoviev has ex-

cellent reasons to concur in the melancholy remark of the former Prime Minister of Great Britain. Communism, it will be remembered, claims to be primarily a scientific doctrine; its policies, we are assured, are based on an objective and impartial investigation of existing conditions; and this gives it immense advantages over any other system of political and economic doctrine. Zinoviev made hardly any contribution to the substantiation of these claims.

On May 1, 1919, there appeared in Moscow the first number of the new mouthpiece of the Communist International, a periodical issued simultaneously in several languages and entitled *Kommunisticheski Internatsional (The Communist International)*. The purpose of the publication was well described by its title and by its frontispiece, which represented a worker breaking the chains encircling the globe. To this first number of the organ of world revolution Zinoviev appropriately contributed an article on *"The Outlook of the Proletarian Revolution."* [6] This characteristic pronouncement, typical of the period, is of considerable interest.

"On March 4, 1919, the Third International was born in Moscow," wrote Zinoviev. "To be more exact, the infant was really born in 1918. . . . When in May, 1918, the Bolshevik Party in Russia, holding full government power, had assumed the name

[6] G. Zinoviev, *Perspektivi proletarskoi revolyutsii (The Outlook of the Proletarian Revolution)*, in *Kommunisticheski Internatsional (The Communist International)*, Moscow-Petrograd, No. 1, May 1, 1919, pp. 37 *sqq*.

of the Russian Communist Party and when a few months later the German Spartacus movement, which already had such a glorious record, had in its turn taken the name of the German Communist Party, it became clear to every revolutionary that the Third International had come into being. In 1919 we had merely to give official recognition to an already existing fact. . . . Now, as we write these lines, the Third International already has as its foundation stones three Soviet republics—those in Russia, in Hungary, and in Bavaria. But no one will be surprised if at the moment when these lines appear in print we will have not three but six or more Soviet republics. Old Europe is dashing at mad speed towards the proletarian revolution. . . . We have, above, assumed that the revolutionary movement in Europe may be limited to the victory of 'democracy.' . . . This assumption is in open contradiction to the facts. It is only too clear to-day that the movement in Europe, on the contrary, is progressing much more rapidly than was anticipated even by the greatest optimists at the Moscow congress of the Third International. When the Hungarian bourgeoisie 'resigned,' this was by no means a merely local development. It was a most characteristic sign of the time. In the historical sense, the whole of the European bourgeoisie is beginning to resign. The victory of communism in Germany is inescapable. Separate defeats will still occur in the near future. Black will, perhaps, still win a victory here and there over red. But final victory will, nevertheless, be to the red; and this in the course of the next months, perhaps even weeks. The movement is proceeding at such terrific speed that we may say with full confidence, within a year we shall already begin to forget that there was a struggle for communism in Europe, because in a year the whole of Europe will be communist. And the struggle for communism will be transferred to America, perhaps to Asia, and to other parts of the world.

"Geographically, the proletarian revolution moves from east to west. This trend of the proletarian revolution is now definitely established. The last events in Turkey have fully confirmed it. Communism won its first victory in Russia. It was due to the fact that the Russian bourgeoisie was weaker, less well organized, than the bourgeoisie in other countries. . . . Why are the French and the Italian bourgeosies the most militant to-day? Because nowhere is the socialist revolution so ripe as it is in France and in Italy. Because the French and Italian capitalists have almost nothing to lose. Only one course is open to them: to break through, to declare war on Russia and Hungary. They try to incite Germany against Russia; in a word, they call surgery to their aid.

"Perhaps we shall see—for a few years, and side by side with communist Europe—American capitalism continue to exist. Perhaps even in England capitalism will continue to exist for a year or two, side by side with communism victorious in the whole of continental Europe. But such co-existences cannot last long. To use the expression of the mouth-piece of the French bourgeoisie, *le Temps,* we may say: capitalist America and communist Europe can-not live together. Certainly not for any length of time. But for the transition period, the possibility of a situation like the one above is not to be ex-cluded. . . .

"The dictatorship of the proletariat is the order of the day in the whole of the civilized world. All our disappointments of to-day will, in a few months, appear utterly insignificant in comparison with the great victories which we shall have won in the mean-time. There is no more durable building than the building of the Third International whose founda-tions were laid in March, 1919. Under the flag of the Third International the working class will be victorious throughout the entire world."

Views similar to those of Zinoviev were expressed by other Bolshevik leaders. "It is perfectly clear now," wrote Bukharin, for instance, "that at the present time there can be no great war that will not sooner or later develop into a world war; and there can be no great revolution that will not affect the whole world, enlist the sympathy of the proletariat, bring upon itself the forces of world imperialism, and develop into a world revolution. . . . Under the existing conditions of world economy and the inter-dependence of its elements, the interdependence of the various states,—organized groups of the bour-geoisie,—it goes without saying that the struggle in one country cannot be successful without the victory of the corresponding combatants in other civilized countries. . . . There is not the slightest doubt that the curve of our economic development will show a sharp upward trend as soon as the technical requirements [the raw materials and fuel denied to Russia by the blockade] will be available. And this is a question of our front, and very largely a question of the development of the world revolution." [7]

These pronouncements of Zinoviev and Bukharin accurately reflected the general attitude of most of the Soviet leaders during the period 1918–1920, an attitude which found its outward manifestation in the creation of the Third International and in the trend of the latter's discussions and policies at its first and second congresses. In the new militant organization of the world proletariat, Zinoviev, it will be remembered, was the president as well as the guiding spirit.

THE THIRD INTERNATIONAL

The Third (Communist) International or Comintern was, as is implied by its name, by no means a new institution. Its predecessors were the First International (1864–1872), established in London by Marx and Engels, and the Second, which came into being in 1889, and, in the opinion of the Soviet leaders, had ceased to exist on the outbreak of the war, or in 1914. The communists believe that the

[7] N. Bukharin, *Diktatura proletariata v Rossii i mirovaya revolyutsya (The Dictatorship of the Proletariat in Russia and the World Revolution)*, in *Kommunisticheski Internatsional*, No. 4, August, 1919, pp. 491–492.

Second International completely failed to fulfil its revolutionary mission, and from an organization for the advancement of the cause of the proletariat against its oppressors degenerated into a mere obedient servant of the bourgeoisie. It is to the First International therefore that they look for inspiration and guidance. The Statute of the Third International adopted by its second congress in July, 1920, includes the following general statement of principles, which is taken from the Statute of the London International of 1864. It proclaims that "the liberation of the working class can be achieved only by the working class itself; that in their struggle for emancipation the workers must strive to create not new privileges and monopolies but to establish equal rights and duties for all, and to abolish all class domination; that the economic dependence of the worker upon the monopolistic owner of the means of production—that is, of all sources of life—is the chief cause of slavery in all its forms, of all social evil, of all spiritual degeneration and of the political inferiority of the working class; that the economic emancipation of the worker is that great purpose to which every political movement must be subordinated, as a means; that all attempts to achieve this purpose have so far remained sterile because of the lack of solidarity among the various kinds of workers in each individual country and the lack of a brotherly union among the workers of different countries; that the emancipation of labor is not a local or national question, but a social

problem which involves the interests of all countries in which there exists the modern social system,
and that it requires for its solution the theoretical
and practical coöperation of the most advanced
countries; that the simultaneous revival of the labor
movement in the industrial countries of Europe
which we observe at the present time, on the one
hand raises new hopes, and on the other serves as a
warning against the repetition of the old mistakes
and necessitates the immediate unification of movements which had no connection in the past." [8] These
purposes the Third International solemnly declared
to be its own, and it promised to bring to a successful conclusion the task undertaken by its predecessor
of 1864.

But if the aims of the Communist International
were similar to those of its precursor and were inherited from the past, the immediate strategical and
tactical problems with which it was confronted, the
means by which the abolition of the bourgeoisie was
to be brought about, were not so clearly defined:
and little guidance could be derived from the short-
lived experience of the First International which,
moveover, operated under entirely different conditions. No serious thought was given to problems
of organization at the first congress of the Comintern in March, 1919. It met, to repeat, in the midst
of the civil war and at a time when the idea of the
inevitability of a communist revolution in at least

[8] *Vtoroi Kongress Kommunisticheskago Internatsionala (The
Second Congress of the Communist International)*, verbatim report, Petrograd, 1921, pp. 619–620.

several advanced European countries was not seriously challenged in Russian Soviet circles. Why should one plan for a protracted period of struggle when it was certain victory was within easy reach? It was at this time that the Zinoviev article we have quoted was written. Europe was like a powder magazine, ready to explode at any moment. The thing to do was to throw in the match that would bring that explosion of world revolution which was everywhere ready and apparent. Then, of course, the Comintern was still in its infancy and the general conditions in Russia were anything but favorable for the making of definite plans for the future.

The first congress of the Comintern therefore limited its activities to revolutionary propaganda in its simplest form. Zinoviev has stated, since, that for the first year of its existence the Comintern was nothing but a society for revolutionary propaganda seeking to disseminate among the masses the ideas of communism.[9] This, he believed, was a great achievement at the time. The first congress issued a manifesto to the proletariat of the world in which it pledged anew the allegiance of its members to the principles laid down in Marx's *Communist Manifesto* of seventy-two years before. The general analysis of the impending downfall of the capitalist system given by Marx was, it maintained, fully justified by the actual course of historical development, although the era of the ultimate struggle came somewhat later than was anticipated by the apostle of

[9] *Ibid.*, p. 193.

world revolution. But it had now arrived. It was the purpose of the new International to do everything in its power to assure the speedy and final victory of communism.[10] In another appeal to the workers of the world the congress embodied the already familiar idea that within a year the whole of Europe would be under the rule of the Soviets.[11] The dictatorship of the proletariat and the establishment of the Soviet form of government were held to offer the only possible method of saving the world from the horrors of that new world war which was inherent in the capitalist system.[12] This was an argument which should have found an easy response in the war-weary Europe of 1919. The proposed organization of the League of Nations was discounted in advance as "the Holy Alliance of the bourgeoisie for the suppression of the proletarian revolution."[13] It was merely a device adopted by the socialists who deserted the ranks of communism to foster counter-revolution in accordance with the orders of their capitalist employers. The workers should not trust any but their own leaders. There was no possible compromise with the bourgeoisie, but only a struggle to a victorious end under the leadership of the Moscow Government and the Moscow International.

[10] *Manifest Kommunisticheskago Internatsional (Manifesto of the Communist International)*, in *Kommunisticheski Internatsional*, No. 1, May 1, 1919, pp. 6–7.

[11] *Kommunisticheski Internatsional*, No. 1, May 1, 1919, p. 25.

[12] See, for instance, *Kommunisticheski Internatsional*, No. 2, July 1, 1919, p. 154.

[13] Resolution on the international situation adopted by the first congress, in *Kommunisticheski Internatsional*, No. 1, May 1, 1919, p. 115.

THE SECOND CONGRESS OF THE COMINTERN

Although the high hopes of the early months of the revolution failed to materialize in the course of 1919 and the first half of 1920, the second congress of the Comintern met in July of that year in a frame of mind not substantially different from that of the first congress. There were certain obvious reasons for optimism. The Soviet Union had succeeded in maintaining itself in face of the concerted opposition of the capitalist world. The civil war, while not yet ended, was well on the way to settlement. The campaign against Poland was in its most promising phase. These were achievements which few would have believed possible on the morrow of the October *coup d'état*. The internal difficulties were still immense, the food situation was getting worse every day, and the international situation was still highly uncertain although it was distinctly better than a year before. And hopes for the speedy overthrow of capitalism were also by no means dead. The world revolution was somewhat slower in coming than was expected at first; but it still seemed to be easily in sight, and was sure to bring in its train the solution of the domestic difficulties of the Soviet Union.

In a speech delivered in Moscow, on March 6, 1920, on the occasion of the first anniversary of the Comintern, Lenin discussed the general international outlook. He expressed the opinion that much had been achieved by the Comintern in the course of of its first year. Immediately after the end of the war, he thought, the situation was extremely favorable to a successful socialist revolution. Its failure to materialize was largely due to a lack of unity in the European proletariat itself and especially to its betrayal by the leaders of the European socialist movement. "If the [Second] International had not been in the hands of traitors who saved the bourgeoisie at the critical moment," he said, "there would have been a very good chance that in many belligerent countries, as well as in some of those that were neutral, where the people were armed, the end of the war would have been followed by revolution, and then the result would have been different." This, however, did not take place, and it would seem to be necessary for the world to travel the same road which Russia travelled between the revolutions of 1905 and 1917 if it was to learn how to lead the masses of the proletariat.[14]

This more sober attitude of Lenin was not without effect upon the work of the second congress of the Comintern, although the enthusiasm for the world revolution was still much in evidence. Zinoviev has given a vivid picture of the general atmosphere which prevailed at this gathering. It was when the Red army was rapidly moving towards Warsaw. A large map of the Russo-Polish front was displayed in the hall where the congress met, and the advancement of the troops was marked on it. "Every morning the delegates with immense interest crowded in

[14] N. Lenin, *Treti Kommunisticheski Internatsional (The Third Communist International)*, in *Kommunisticheski Internatsional*, No. 10, 1920, p. 1453.

front of the map," said Zinoviev. "This was to a certain extent symbolic. The best representatives of the international proletariat, holding their breath, one might say with halting pulses, followed every advance of our troops, and all clearly understood that the fulfilment of the military task would mean the speeding up of the international revolution. All knew that the fate of the international proletarian revolution literally depended, at that time, on every forward move of our Red army." [15] No wonder that under these conditions the immediate prospects of world revolution were still the chief concern of the delegates.

Nevertheless certain concessions were made to the inescapable realities of the existing political situation. Zinoviev frankly admitted that his revolutionary enthusiasm of a year earlier had carried him too far. Referring to his article which we have quoted he remarked that the term of life given by him to the capitalist world was somewhat too short. The creation of an international Soviet republic controlled by the Comintern would take not a few weeks or months, as he originally thought, but two or perhaps even three years. This was, however, as far as he was willing to go in the summer of 1920. [16]

It was at the second congress of the Comintern

[15] Zinoviev's report on the work of the Communist International in *Desyati Sezd Rossiskoi Kommunisticheskoi Partii (Tenth Congress of the Russian Communist Party)*, March 8–16, 1921, verbatim report, Petrograd, 1921, p. 187.

[16] *Vtoroi Kongress Kommunisticheskago Internatsionala (The Second Congress of the Communist International)*, verbatim report, Petrograd, 1921, p. 16.

that Lenin forcibly advanced his theory that the capitalist stage of development was not inevitable for backward countries which had entered upon the path of progress since the war. It might be avoided altogether if the Soviet Governments of the more advanced countries would come to their assistance with all the means at their disposal, and the victorious proletariat carried on, among the backward nations, a well-organized campaign of propaganda. Lenin declared that it was the duty of the Comintern not only to create communist organizations among colonial peoples and educate them in the right spirit; it was also its duty to furnish the theoretical foundation for the policy to be followed in backward countries. This theoretical foundation was the principle that colonial nations can pass to communism without going through the capitalistic stage.[17] It was embodied in the resolutions of the congress.

Much of the time of the congress was devoted to questions of the organization of centralized communist parties as a necessary preliminary to a victorious struggle against capitalism. Zinoviev, after describing the Comintern of 1919 as a society for revolutionary propaganda, declared that it must be rebuilt as a "militant organization of the international proletariat." The second congress had the task of transforming the Third International into a fighting unit capable not only of spreading communist ideas, but also of assuring the application

[17] *Ibid.*, pp. 110–120.

of these ideas in practice. The First International, he said, was a highly centralized institution which attempted to control and direct every economic strike. This was possible to a certain extent because the labor movement was still in its infancy; it was young and weak. No such rigid centralization was, of course, practicable under modern conditions when the labor movement had grown into one of the great factors in the life of the world. The Second International, on the contrary, was a rather loosely knit body, lacking real direction or control from the centre. Using the Hegelian formula, Zinoviev characterized them as the thesis and the antithesis. The Third International must be the synthesis, the culminating point of the entire process of historical development. It must be the International of action, it must be the instrument of struggle in time of peace as well as during the uprising, and after it the rallying point for that portion of the international proletariat which was conscious of its historic mission and was willing to fight for it.[18] Intervening in the debates at a later stage, Zinoviev proclaimed that the historical rôle of the Communist Party consisted in leading the masses, and not in waiting until the masses push it forward. "We have waited long enough," he said. "The working class has waited long enough. The moment for the decisive struggle has now arrived." [19]

[18] *Ibid.*, pp. 194–196.
[19] *Ibid.*, p. 324.

These ideas found their expression in the resolutions of the second congress and in the Statute of the Third International which, it will be remembered, was adopted by the second congress. "The Communist International," said one of the resolutions, "is the concentrated will of the revolutionary proletariat of the world. Its mission consists in the organization of the working class of the whole world for the overthrow of the capitalist system and the establishment of communism. The Third International is a militant unit which must unite the revolutionary forces of the world." [20]

Article I of the Statute defined the aims of the Comintern with even greater precision: "The New International Brotherhood of Workers is founded for the joint action of the proletarians of various countries who in common aim to overthrow capitalism and establish the dictatorship of the proletariat and the international Soviet republic for the destruction of class society and the introduction of socialism, that first stage of communist society." [21] The preamble to the Statute further amplified this statement: "The Communist International has for its purpose the struggle by all available means, including armed force, for the overthrow of the international bourgeoisie and the creation of an international Soviet republic as a transition stage to the complete abolition of the state." [22] The dictatorship

[20] *Ibid.*, p. 604.
[21] *Ibid.*, p. 621.
[22] *Ibid.*, p. 620.

of the proletariat, coupled with the Soviet form of government, was again set forth as offering the only method for saving the world from the horrors of the capitalist system. A manifesto issued by the second congress solemnly announced that "the Communist International has adopted the cause of Soviet Russia as its own cause. The international proletariat will not lay down its sword until Soviet Russia has become a link in the federation of the Soviet republics of the world." [23]

Considering the general trend of the debates of the second congress and its resolutions, it seems reasonably clear that they did not differ substantially in their essence and tone from those of the first congress. It was still the "heroic" period of the Bolshevik revolution when the transformation of the world into a communist commonwealth was believed to be a thing if not exactly of to-morrow, then at the worst, of the very near future. Looking back on those eventful years from the more sober atmosphere of 1922, Zinoviev admitted that the Comintern of the first and second congress failed correctly to appraise the existing situation. Every labor disturbance, almost every strike, was held to be the beginning of the final struggle in which capitalism was to find its doom. While defending the theoretical work accomplished by the second congress, Zinoviev recognized that the general attitude of its leaders was very much the same as it was in March, 1919. The common belief in the imminence of the world

[23] *Ibid.*, p. 647.

revolution still largely dominated the proceedings.[24]
It was not until 1921 that the defeat of these hopes
was reluctantly conceded.

THE CONGRESS OF EASTERN PEOPLES

One of the most ambitious enterprises undertaken
in the fulfilment of the ideas which dominated Russian Communist circles during that period was the
Congress of the Eastern Peoples called in Baku in
September, 1920. Lenin attached very great importance to the part of the colonial and backward
countries in bringing about the downfall of capitalism. The weakest link of the capitalist chain was
surely in the colonies where national uprisings
against the foreign oppressors could be easily di-
verted into the channels of socialist revolution. And
Zinoviev had declared, as we have seen, that "geographically, the proletarian revolution proceeds from
east to west. This trend of the proletarian revolution," he said, "is now definitely established." Again
the salvation of the world was to come from the East.

A Soviet writer, discussing the peculiar position
of Russia as a kind of clearing house between Europe
and Asia, quoted the well-known saying of A. I.
Herzen that "Europeans consider that Russia belongs to Asia; and the people in Asia look upon
Russia as belonging to Europe." Such was the position of Russia under the tsars when, he argues, she

[24] *Odinnadtsati Sezd Rossiskoi Kommunisticheskoi Partii Bolshevikov (The Eleventh Congress of the Russian Communist
Bolshevik Party)*, 22 March–2 April, 1922; verbatim report, Moscow, 1922, pp. 187–188.

played in Europe the part of international police-
man, and in Asia she carried on the policy of
European imperialism. This situation still exists,
even after the Bolshevik revolution, although Russia
now appears in a very different rôle. Capitalist
Europe looks upon her as the breeding centre of
the "Asiatic plague of Bolshevism," while in the
East she has assumed the novel part of the standard
bearer of ideas of the European communist revolution.[25] It was to the East, with its infinite complexity
of social relationship and its survivals of feudalism
and of tribal and patriarchal organization, that the
communist leaders turned with much hope.

The first thing to do was to prove to the peoples
of the East that the U.S.S.R. was their real friend
and that, unlike the capitalist countries of Europe,
she was concerned with their welfare and wanted
nothing for herself. In June, 1919, the Soviet Government sent a note to Persia in which it cancelled
all Persian debts to the Russian Imperial Government, voided all Russian concessions, transferred to
the Persian people the Russian Bank in Persia, with
Persia's railroads, electric-power stations, and the
like. The capitulations were also abolished. Karakhan, who signed the note on behalf of the Government of Moscow, urged Persia to obtain similar
"compensations" from Great Britain. A like attitude was adopted by the Soviets toward other Asiatic
people. After this groundwork had been successfully

[25] G. Safarov, *Vostok i revolyutsya (The East and the Revolution),* in *Kommunisticheski Internatsional,* No. 15, 1920, pp.
3130 *sqq.*

laid down, the Communist International proceeded to carry out the ambitious plan of organizing an uprising of the Asiatic nations against their western oppressors. Its most important step was the Congress of Eastern Peoples which met in Baku on September 1, 1920.

The Congress was called by the Executive Committee of the Communist International. It was attended by 1,891 delegates representing thirty-two national groups. Zinoviev was unanimously elected president. The Congress discussed the general political situation, national, colonial, and agrarian problems, Soviet government for the East, and questions of organization. Zinoviev and Radek opened the proceedings and called for a struggle against the imperialistic policy of the Entente, for a holy war of the exploited masses of the East against the tyranny of the foreigner. Zinoviev pointed out that in his opinion the East was not yet ripe for communism, and that therefore the Comintern was willing for the present to coöperate with the nationalist-democratic and revolutionary elements, while supporting the still weak communist movement among the Eastern peoples.

Although the Congress received the Russian communists with much enthusiasm and passed the militant resolutions proposed by them, including a resolution on the agrarian question which demanded the abolition of large estates without compensation and of all feudal privileges, and also expressed itself in favor of a Soviet system of government for Eastern countries, the triumph of the Comintern was not quite so complete as was expected. It soon transpired that the members of the Congress were divided into two groups—the communists and the far larger group of non-party delegates. The latter again, Zinoviev conceded in his report to the Executive Committee of the Comintern, included delegates who actually did not belong to any political party, such as the representatives of the peasants and of the semi-proletarian urban population, and also a number of individuals who, although they described themselves as having no party allegiance, really represented the bourgeoisie. One of them, a Turkish professor and a member of the "Union and Progress" group, declared that arms were all they wanted from Russia. Answering Zinoviev's question, whether the Turks knew what the Bolsheviks really are, Enver Pasha replied that the Turks said that "a Bolshevik is a man who is an enemy of England." "And what do they think about the Bolsheviks fighting against the capitalists and the landlords?" was Zinoviev's next question. "That is a matter in which the Turks are not interested," was the answer to that.

Some disappointment was undoubtedly caused the Russian communists by the kind of permanent organization which the Congress decided to establish. The original proposal for the creation of an instrument that would control all Soviet formations in the East and also act as a central executive board and court of appeal was defeated. Instead, the Congress decided to organize a "Council of Propaganda and

Action of the Eastern Peoples," and its functions were not clearly defined. It was to consist of forty-five members, and was to meet in Baku at least every three months. But little has been heard of it since 1920.[26] While the Congress of the Eastern People was officially described as "the first congress," it has not had any second meeting. Revolution in the East was just as slow in coming as it was in western Europe.

It took time for the leaders of the communist movement to reconcile themselves to the delay. In a speech delivered by Zinoviev at a meeting of the Independent German Party in Halle in October, 1920, he emphasized the immense importance attached by the Third International to the revolution in the East. "If Marx once said that a European revolution without England would be merely a tempest in a teacup, then we will tell you, German comrades, that a proletarian revolution without Asia will not be a world revolution. . . . At the Baku congress we discovered the element that in the past was missing in the proletarian movement. We discovered what is essential to the realization of world revolution. The oppressed masses of Asia must awaken. . . . I must make a confession: when in Baku I beheld hundreds of Persians and Turks join us in singing 'The International' I felt my eyes fill with tears and I recognized the breathing of the world revolution. Yes, I stress it, not merely the European, but the

[26] *Iz protokolov Ispolkoma Kominterna (From the Minutes of the Executive Committee of the Comintern),* in *Kommunisticheski Internatsional,* No. 14, 1920, pp. 2941 *sqq.*

world revolution. We have here the rising of all the oppressed peoples of the world against capitalism." [27] The day, however, was not far distant when a more sober attitude was to prevail in the leading circles of the Communist Party and the Comintern.

THE SOVIET GOVERNMENT AND THE COMINTERN

The policy of open propaganda for ideas of world revolution was not to be without its inconvenience; and the Soviet Government learned this from bitter experience. The first step was the blockade of Russia by the Allied and Associated Powers immediately after the great war; and following that came the support lent by the capitalist nations to the White troops in the Russian civil war. There is little doubt that the unfriendly action of the Allied governments was inspired, on the one hand, by a general failure to realize at that time that the communist rule in Russia was something which had come to stay, and, on the other, by the greatly exaggerated fears which the inflammatory propaganda broadcast from Moscow inspired in the capitals of Europe and America. As months passed and the world revolution failed to materialize, it became increasingly important for the new Russian government to find a solution which would allow it to continue its revolutionary work among the nations of the world, and at the same time pave the way for a resumption of

[27] G. Zinoviev, *Mirovaya revolyutsya i Kommunisticheski Internatsional (World Revolution and the Communist International)*, a speech delivered at the meeting of the German Independent Party in Halle on October 4, 1920, Petrograd, 1921.

relations with other countries. This solution was found in the convenient, if much disputed, doctrine that the Third International was independent of the Soviet Government. This doctrine did not find its full expression until a later period. It had figured prominently in the conflicts that arose between the Soviet Union and the various European governments, especially the British, which had particularly good reasons to be concerned with the effects of communist propaganda among the colonial and semi-colonial nations. And it was doctrine that, during the period now under discussion, had already been outlined. It consists, as everybody knows, in the flat statement that there is no connection between the governing body of the Union and the Third International; that the latter is an entirely independent organization, and that the part taken in its work by the Soviet leaders is a purely private activity with which the government is in no way concerned and for which it cannot be held responsible. A perfectly good case can be made, and has been made on several occasions, to show that the Russian Communist Party controls both the Soviet Government and the Third International, and that the latter's being independent of the former is nothing but an empty legal fiction.

It may be argued, on the other hand, that legal fictions represent devices the use of which in the field of international affairs is by no means limited to the policies of that ill-bred newcomer in the diplomatic arena, the Russian Bolshevik. A familiar ex-

ample is the contention which has been consistently
advanced by successive governments in Washington
that there is no connection between the question of
inter-Allied debts and that of reparations. Europe,
of course, never accepted this point of view, but she
bowed to the desire firmly expressed by the great
creditor nation with the result that some curious
international documents came into existence. Such
is, for instance, the well-known "Concurrent Memo-
randum, but not a Part of the Report," attached to
the Young Plan, which provided for the benefits
Germany was to derive from a possible scaling down
of the payments the Allied countries owed to the
United States. This document not only does not mention the United States, but even avoids any direct
reference to inter-Allied debts which are modestly
disguised under the noncommittal, if transparent,
name of "out-payments." At times, too, there has
been like criticism of the general policy of Washington with reference to the question of the recognition
of the Soviet Union. It is a fact of common knowledge that a large number of American citizens are
visiting Russia, and that Soviet citizens are permitted to enter this country; that many American engineers and technical experts are actively employed
by the Soviet Government in carrying on its plan of
industrialization; that official Soviet agencies such
as the Amtorg and the Information Bureau in Washington, camouflaged as American corporations, are
operating on the soil of the United States. It is also

known that on the suggestion of the government at
Washington the Soviet Government was invited by
France to join the so-called Briand-Kellogg Pact
and that it actually accepted the invitation. In the
opinion of one of America's leading international
lawyers, who cannot be suspected of pro-communist
sympathies, this constituted "implied recognition." [28]
In spite of this, the official attitude of Washington
toward Russia remained unchanged and, at the
present writing, the largest country in Europe and
its government, which has maintained itself in office for fifteen years and is not likely to disappear,
are still officially nonexistent, so far as the President
and the Congress of the United States are concerned.[29] Is this not just as flagrant a departure from

[28] John Bassett Moore, *Candor and Common Sense*, New York,
1930, p. 13: "We had entered into an international agreement
commonly called the Kellogg Pact, to which the Soviet Government, upon the solicitation of one of our co-signers, had, with
our full knowledge and acquiescence, been permitted to adhere.
By this act we necessarily recognized the Soviet Government;
for, by the hornbooks—the very primers of the kindergartens—
of international law and diplomacy, recognition may be implied
as well as express, and one of the stock examples of implied
recognition is the entrance into conventional relations."

[29] The Appellate Division of the Supreme Court of New York
has expressed a somewhat different opinion. "While it is true
that the United States Government, for reasons which it deems
sufficient, has failed to establish diplomatic relations with the
existing Soviet Government in Russia or to recognize said government as a de jure government, nevertheless it has recognized
the de facto existence of the Russian Soviet Government." (M.
Salimoff & Co. vs. Standard Oil Co., New York Supplement, Vol.
262, No. 6, April 11, 1933, p. 695.) It would seem that the point
of view of the Supreme Court of the State of New York has
been endorsed by President Roosevelt when he addressed his
message on disarmament of May 16, 1933, direct to the head of
the Soviet state, M. Kalinin.

the world of realities into the world of fiction as the refusal of the Soviet Government to acknowledge its connection with the Third International?

One of the early statements of the attitude of the Soviet Government toward the Third International was given in an interesting article published in October, 1919, by the aristocratic People's Commissar for Foreign Affairs, George Chicherin.[30] He argued that the activities of the Second International, in the last resort, were nothing but the diplomacy of the proletariat, as distinct from the diplomacy of governments. The aims of proletarian foreign policy consisted in opposing the foreign policy of the ruling bourgeoisie; that is, in waging the class struggle on an international scale. An entirely new situation, however, has been created by the appearance of Soviet governments. (In those early days, the Soviet writers and statesmen never missed an opportunity to use the term "Soviet government" in the plural!) For the first time after a long interval the revolutionary proletariat is, in its foreign policy, being confronted with positive aims: the support and strengthening of the revolutionary proletarian governments, which are its natural strongholds, in the world struggle of the oppressed against the oppressors. But if the course of conduct to be followed by the revolutionary parties and their leader, the Third International, is perfectly plain, the position of the

[30] Chicherin, *Mezhdunarodnaya politika dvukh internatsionalov (The Foreign Policy of the Two Internationals),* in *Kommunisticheski Internatsional,* October, 1919, No. 6.

Soviet governments is not quite so simple. "As governments actually existing side by side with other governments," wrote Chicherin, "they are forced to enter into certain relations with the latter, and these relations impose upon them duties which must be taken into consideration. The Commissar for Foreign Affairs, writing for the columns of the organ of the Third International, must take into consideration the fact that he is to a certain extent bound by his office in the government, which is no longer in the position of a revolutionary party without governmental responsibilities."[31] Revolutionary governments are in opposition to bourgeois governments. They cannot participate in their imperialistic undertakings. And their purpose is to live in peace with all other countries. They must be ready to defend themselves against capitalist aggression. At the same time, however, they must also refrain from any aggressive policy. "The rôle of Soviet diplomacy is strictly defensive, but it is also a highly responsible one," wrote the Commissar for Foreign Affairs. "When we speak therefore of the positive aims of the Third International, we must not identify with the communist parties the Soviet governments controlled by them."[32] Chicherin made no further attempt to elaborate the ground for the distinction between the communist parties and the Soviet governments controlled by such parties and he probably acted wisely, as a mere declaratory statement of a controversial

[31] *Ibid.*, p. 825.
[32] *Ibid.*, p. 826.

principle is more effective than a poor and vulnerable argument. On the other hand, he took pains to explain that the policies of the Soviet governments are always opposed to those of the capitalist states, inasmuch as the Soviet governments defend the interests of the exploited masses and especially the right of colonial peoples to self-determination. The limits of the restrictions imposed upon the Soviet governments by their international position vary with the changes in the political situation. For instance, the policy of direct appeal for a world revolution carried on by the Soviet government in the first months of its rule was fully justified, in his opinion, by the immense effect it produced. In spite of the limitations to which the activities of the Soviet governments are subject, they form the very centre of the international policies of the left wing of the international labor movement. Like the Second International, the Third International has a foreign policy of its own; but it is no longer a purely negative policy, but one which has definite constructive purposes made possible by the existence of Soviet governments. While not forgetting its general aims in the more advanced capitalist countries, the Third International must by all available means advance the establishment of Soviet republics in colonial countries; and this is made possible by the decline of the capitalist system. It is the broader general program of the Third International directed toward the world revolution which permits the definition of its immediate concrete aims.

The general trend of the argument presented by the Commissar for Foreign Affairs, it will be readily admitted, was hardly of a nature to inspire much confidence on the part of the capitalist nations in the sincerity of his contention that there is no connection between the government of the Union and the Comintern. Nevertheless, he laid down the foundations of a doctrine of which Moscow made frequent use in the years to come.

LENIN'S WARNING

It would be, of course, a mistake to imagine that Lenin was not affected by the general expectation of the immediate outbreak of the world revolution, which prevailed about the Kremlin in 1918–1920. He admitted, for instance, to Clara Zetkin that the failure of the Polish campaign was partly due to mistaken political judgment: he and the Soviet Government put their hope in the Polish revolution which failed to materialize.[33] But it is characteristic of this theorist and philosopher of the revolution that he was by no means blind to the great difficulties which Russia had to face and to overcome if it was to achieve its ultimate aim—the classless communite of the future. In the early part of 1919, at the very time when Zinoviev made his most extravagant claims, Lenin submitted the whole course of the Russian revolution to a careful analysis, which led him to certain conclusions. He pointed out that

[63] Louis Fischer, *The Soviets in World Affairs,* New York, 1930, Vol. I, pp. 270–271.

while for a number of reasons it had proved easier for the Russian proletariat to inaugurate the revolution than it would have been for the proletariat of more advanced countries, the final victory of socialism in Russia presents exceptionally great difficulties. Among the reasons which facilitated the establishment of the dictatorship of the proletariat in Russia, Lenin pointed to the extraordinary backwardness of tsardom, which greatly stimulated the revolutionary energy of the masses. This backwardness of the country permitted an unusually favorable combination. The proletarian revolutions against the bourgeoisie and the peasant revolution against the landlords could work as one, a combination foreseen by Marx as early as 1856, when he discussed the possibility of a proletarian revolution supported by a peasant war in Prussia. Another factor of great importance was the revolutionary outburst of 1905 in Russia, which proved to be a kind of dress rehearsal for 1917. It played an immense part in educating the masses and was, indeed, a necessary preliminary without which the *coup d'état* of October could not have succeeded. The geographical position of Russia allowed her to withstand the concerted action of the capitalist powers for a longer period than would have been possible for many other countries. Lenin also believed that the peculiar relationship which existed in Russia between the proletariat and the peasantry placed the former in a position of leadership which facilitated the transition from a bourgeois to a socialist revolution. And he claimed that long experience in revolutionary work and lessons from mass labor movements in western Europe paved the way for the creation of so peculiar a form of government as the Soviets. But if victory came to the proletariat of Russia with relative ease, the road it would have to travel before it reached the final goal would be a long and thorny one. The technical backwardness of the country and her low educational standards were the chief obstacles which could not be overcome without a protracted and sustained effort. Therefore the more advanced European countries, in which the proletariat was more numerous and influential, all had chances to outdistance Russia, provided they took the same road, the dictatorship of the proletariat.[34]

The real wisdom of this warning was not fully appreciated until the "heroic" period of the Bolshevist revolution, the period which saw Trotsky and Zinoviev at the zenith of their power and influence, was over. The capitalist world not only survived the first and vigorous onslaught of communism, but also emerged from the struggle without heavy losses. The propaganda method of bringing about the revolution was obviously not enough. The Third International and the communist movement were confronted with the urgent problem of revising their tactics.

[34] N. Lenin, *Treti internatsional i ego mesto v istorii (The Third International and Its Place in History)*, in *Kommunisticheski Internatsional*, No. 1, 1919, pp. 35–36.

CHAPTER III

LOW TIDE, 1921-1924

THE END OF THE CIVIL WAR

The year 1920 brought considerable and important changes in the international position of the Soviet Union. Some of them were distinctly favorable
to the newly born republic of the proletariat. The
so-called White armies, consisting of anti-Bolshevik
Russians, one after another rapidly collapsed, and
thus disclosed how completely lacking in all real foundation was the whole movement. Its ultimate failure
was made particularly striking by the easy victories
won over the Reds in the course of 1918 and the first
half of 1919, when the troops of Denikin, Miller,
Kolchak, and Yudenich were pressing back the Bolsheviks and advancing toward Moscow from the
north, south, east, and west. Many were those
among the White Russians and their friends in
European capitals who in those days believed in the
imminent breakdown of the Soviet rule, and believed
in it with the same unchangeable fanaticism with
which Zinoviev and his followers believed the world
revolution would come within the next few weeks;
but the counter-revolutionary hopes also failed to
materialize. The second half of 1919 and 1920 saw
the complete and final defeat of the White armies.

Kolchak, Yudenich, Miller, Denikin, and his successor, Wrangel, all bit the dust. At the end of October, 1920, the last remnants of Wrangel's troops in the south, totalling, with the civilians, some 150,000, left Russian shores and sailed from the Crimea for Constantinople, and a further destination unknown at the time. Thus closed one of the most tragic pages in the unhappy history of those eventful years. We are not here concerned with the causes of this failure. It seems probable that the ill-fated anti-Bolshevist movement was inevitable at the time, and was a spontaneous protest against the communist rule; but it is also clear to-day that it never had any chance of success. Its inherent weakness has been frankly stated by one of its most respected leaders, General Wrangel. "The population," he writes, "greeted our army with wild enthusiasm; they had all suffered from the Bolsheviki, and only wanted to be allowed to live in peace, and yet they had to endure the horrors of pillage, violence and despotism all over again. Result: confusion at the front and risings in the interior. . . . The war is becoming to some a means of growing rich; reëquipment has degenerated into pillage and peculation. . . . The army is absolutely demoralized, and is fast becoming a collection of tradesmen and profiteers." [1] As to the commanding officers, they were devoting their energies to intrigues, quarrels, and not infrequently to debauchery.

[1] *The Memoirs of General Wrangel*, translated by Sophie Goulston, New York, 1930, pp. 112-113.

The collapse of the White movement necessitated a revision on the part of the Allies of their attitude toward Russia. On January 16, 1920, the Supreme Council cancelled the economic blockade of Russia which had been declared soon after the Armistice. The Allied troops were gradually withdrawn from Archangel, Odessa, the Caucasus, and other parts of Russian territory. The Russo-Polish War also came to an end in October, 1920, and a peace treaty between the two countries—a very onerous one from the Russian point of view—was formally signed in Riga on March 18, 1921. Europe was slowly awakening to the unpleasant fact that the Union of the Soviet Socialist Republics had come to stay.

Moscow had every reason to be satisfied with the strengthening of its international position, although its success was purchased at a price. The economic disorganization of the country was complete and had reached a stage when it not only inflicted terrible sufferings upon the population, but even threatened the political existence of the Soviet state, as was made clear by the uprisings which took place in various parts of the country and among which that of Tambov was, in particular, notable for its ruthless brutality. Serious cases of disaffection also occurred among the troops, including a mutiny of the sailors of the fortress of Kronstadt, that stronghold of the revolution. Some drastic revision of domestic policy was obviously necessary if even worse outbreaks were to be avoided.

No less unsatisfactory, from the point of view of

the Moscow government, was the general trend of world events. It is true that the Soviet Union succeeded in maintaining itself for a much longer period than most of even its warmest admirers would have expected at the end of 1917 and in 1918; and it had won a rather startling victory over the much-advertised leaders of the White movement, backed by the governments of the Allied Powers. But this triumph came in a manner which was unforeseen and in a sense unwelcome to the Russian communists. The establishment of a socialist republic in one country alone, and especially in a backward peasant country like Russia, created a situation which it was not easy to reconcile with the general scheme of Karl Marx and his disciples. The downfall of capitalism, it was assumed in those days, was to come through the simultaneous or almost simultaneous revolution in at least several of the most advanced countries. This idea, as we have seen, dominated the "heroic" period of the Bolshevist revolution which came to a close with the defeat and withdrawal of the White troops. From this point of view the successful defense of the existence of the Soviet Union was hardly an adequate compensation for the failure of the socialist revolution in the more advanced countries as well as in the East. In 1921 it was no longer possible to speak of "Soviet governments" in the plural. The communist rule of Bela Kun in Hungary collapsed in the summer of 1919, a failure for which the intransigent policy of the Hungarian communists toward the peasantry was held responsible. Just as disappointing proved to be the German revolution which, under the leadership of the German Social-Democratic Party, sought arrangements with the Allies instead of forming an "invincible revolutionary bloc" with its eastern neighbor.[2] The overthrow of the monarchies of the Hohenzollerns and the Habsburgs with the score of smaller dynasties it brought in its train was cold comfort when compared with the disappointment of greater hopes. Whether the countries of Europe were ruled by monarchs or by democratic parliaments did not really matter from the point of view of the communist. The important thing was that the democratic revolutions in the central empires failed to merge into socialist revolutions, in spite of the exceedingly favorable conditions created by the misery, discontent, and weariness brought about by the war.

Hope that the outbreak of the socialist revolution among the European nations would come soon was not, of course, abandoned at once. The political horizon was still carefully scrutinized for any signs of the great conflagration which was to engulf capitalism. Zinoviev, the great "romantic" of the world revolution, was among those who found it particularly difficult to become reconciled to the hard facts. In his speech at the meeting of the German Independent Party in Halle, in October, 1920, he still forcibly advanced the opinion that there was no reason to think that world revolution had been post-

---

[2] Verbatim report of the second congress of the Communist International, p. 647.

poned for an indefinite period. On the contrary, he maintained all the economic premises for a final victory of socialism were in existence. He confessed that the transition to socialism had proved more difficult than was anticipated, and that it had brought to the working classes much suffering and misery. Nevertheless, civil war was the only method by which the exploited classes could shake off the yoke of their oppressors. The failure of world revolution to materialize was not due to any conditions inherent in the situation, but to the lack of enthusiasm, faith, vision, and confidence among the leaders of the revolutionary parties outside Russia. In his opinion, there was no ground for pessimism, and he proceeded to enumerate the many bright spots on the revolutionary horizon where his expert eyes detected signs of the approaching social cataclysm. Most important among them was the formation of the "Council of Action" in England which he interpreted as the nucleus of a proletarian government. In Italy, a proletarian revolution had already begun and had found its expression in the seizing of factories by the Soviets of Workers and the formation of Red guards. Austria, too, was in such a state that no one would have been surprised if to-morrow's newspapers announced that a Soviet government had been set up there. The same was true of the Balkans, which were completely ripe for a socialist revolution.[3]

These pronouncements by Zinoviev failed to up-

[3] G. Zinoviev, *Mirovaya revolyutsya i Kommunisticheski Internatsional (World Revolution and the Communist International)*, pp. 10, 12, 13, 14, 20, 22.

lift his German audience in Halle; and even in Russia they were no longer received with the enthusiasm of the early months of 1919. Whatever effect they might have produced was soon destroyed by the merciless course of events which paid no attention to the predictions of the head of the Third International. The English Council of Action did not grow into a second government functioning side by side with the Parliament at Westminster. Italy, instead of turning communist, evolved the new doctrine of fascism which is rightly considered by the Bolshevists as their worst enemy. Austria continued to struggle along under a bourgeois government and refused to follow the lead of Moscow in spite of the heavy economic handicaps imposed upon it by the peace treaties. Revolution in the Balkans failed to materialize. The danger and inconvenience of too much use of the future tense had once more been demonstrated.

THE TURN IN THE ROAD

The year 1921 is an important landmark in the history of the Soviet Union. The determining factors which called for a revision of the policy of Moscow were, on the one hand, the collapse of the White movement and the resultant strengthening of the international position of the first communist state; and, on the other, the failure of the socialist revolution in the more advanced countries to materialize. The situation thus created, as we know, was not foreseen by the leaders of the communist movement and necessitated a readjustment of their attitude in both domestic and foreign matters. The domestic policy of the Moscow government in 1918–1920 was characterized by the same uncompromising spirit which we have observed in international relations. It is generally known as the system of "War Communism," and it provided for the taking over by the government of all national activities and the socialization of even the smaller industrial enterprises. The peasants who, for political reasons, were not only permitted to take over and divide among themselves the large estates but were even strongly encouraged to do so—thus giving satisfaction to the desires they had cherished and suppressed since the days of the emancipation of 1861—were made subject to ruthless requisitions and a régime approaching that of hard labor. This extreme policy was forced upon the Moscow government by the course of events, and was embarked upon as a measure of expediency against the better judgment of some of its greatest leaders, among whom was Lenin. The Left Wing communists, on the contrary, saw in War Communism the realization of their dream and clamored for further and more drastic steps. Trotsky advocated the militarization of labor, which he planned to reorganize along the lines of the Red army. The complete abolition of money was suggested, and the introduction of a "unit of labor" as the universal measure of value was discussed in January, 1920. The period of War Communism, which was characterized by rigid centralization, the abolition of the market, and state-organized barter, resulted not only in the breakdown of the economic machinery of the country, but also in a widespread dissatisfaction with the policy of the government which found its expression, as we know, in peasant uprisings and mutinies among the troops. The latter were largely explained by the fact that Russia is a predominantly agricultural country and that therefore any Russian army—Imperial, White, or Red— was *par excellence* a peasant army, being, as such, bound to the agricultural community by close and innumerable ties. The régime of ruthless requisitions to which the peasants were subjected naturally could not leave the Red soldiers indifferent.[4]

The truly intolerable situation created by War Communism was brought to an end in the spring of 1921 by the introduction of the so-called New Economic Policy which relieved the pressure of centralization, restored the market, permitted a certain amount of domestic trading by private individuals, gave some encouragement to private initiative in industry, and replaced the requisitions of the peasants' grain first by a tax in kind and later by a tax in money. The introduction of the New Economic Policy, which was looked upon at the time with many misgivings and was severely criticized by the Left Wing communists, was very largely the achievement of Lenin, who defended it on the ground that it offered the needed "breathing space." It has

[4] For an excellent discussion of War Communism and of the New Economic Policy, *see* Maurice Dobb, *Russian Economic Development since the Revolution*, New York, 1928.

been recognized since by communist writers as one
of the most striking manifestations of Lenin's revolutionary genius. The usual argument in defense of
the New Economic Policy is not limited to the recognition of its necessity as a mere measure of expediency. The point is also made that although the New
Economic Policy restored certain forms of capitalism
which were eliminated under War Communism, it
nevertheless did not signify a return to capitalism.
The essential difference between capitalism and
socialism under the New Economic Policy is that political power in the latter case is vested in the proletariat, and it also controls all the more important industries. Under these conditions there is no class
exploitation, and therefore there is no capitalism, although its forms survive. The growth of state capitalism in a proletarian country means the strengthening of the working class, not of the bourgeoisie. The
New Economic Policy should not be interpreted as
the abandonment of the world revolution, but merely
as an adaptation of Russia's policy to a slower
tempo.[5]

A somewhat analogous change took place in the
international policy of the Soviet Union. The forcible propaganda for an immediate world revolution
in the field of foreign affairs was not in a sense unlike
the application of the methods of War Communism

[5] *Chetverti Vsemirni Kongress Kommunisticheskago Internatsionala (The Fourth World Congress of the Communist International),* selected reports and resolutions, Moscow–Petrograd,
1923, pp. 96, 104 (Trotsky's report on the New Economic Policy
and the outlook for world revolution).

to domestic problems. Both were dictated by the exigencies of the international situation and both gave expression to the boisterous enthusiasm of the more extreme elements of a victorious revolutionary party. The new situation in which the Soviet Union found itself in 1921 called for revision of her attitude toward the outside world just as it necessitated the substitution of the New Economic Policy for War Communism. The first assault of the revolutionary proletariat upon international capitalism fell short of its objective; but the attacking army was not wiped out of existence or its spirit broken. What it needed was time, a "breathing space." Communism was willing to make important concessions to the exigencies of the moment, but not to surrender its final aim. It was a policy of *reculer pour mieux sauter*.

The new attitude of the Soviet government was clearly outlined by Lenin at the tenth congress of the Communist Party which met in Moscow on March 8–16, 1921. Lenin there pointed out that help from the western European countries was coming, but that it was coming more slowly than was originally expected.[6] On the other hand, there was no doubt that world revolution had made immense progress as compared with the situation a year before. This was largely due to the activities of the Comintern, which had grown, since its second congress, into a real factor in the policies of every important European country.

[6] This was regretfully admitted even by Zinoviev in his report to the congress.

Until the second congress it had been hardly more than a proclamation, but now communist parties had sprung up in Germany, France, Italy. This indicates the rapid growth of the proletarian movement, accompanied by an intensification of the economic crisis in the capitalist world. "But in any case," Lenin added, "if we had drawn from this the conclusion that help would come from there [western Europe] within a short time in the shape of a lasting proletarian revolution, we should have been mere lunatics and I feel sure that there is no one in this hall who has such views. We have learned in the course of the last three years that our stake in international revolution does not mean that we expect it to materialize within a definite period of time, that the pace of development, which is growing more and more rapid, may or may not bring revolution in the spring, and that therefore we must coördinate our activities with the relationships existing among the various classes in our own country and abroad, in order thereby to maintain for a protracted period the dictatorship of the proletariat and to free ourselves, even if gradually, of all the misfortunes, and the effects of the crises which have befallen us. Only such an attitude will be sound and sober." [7] Lenin then went on to say that already the policy of the Moscow government had for some time been directed toward the establishment of peaceful relations with the outside world. An important step in

[7] *Desyati Sezd Rossiskoi Kommunisticheskoi Partii (Tenth Congress of the Russian Communist Party)*, verbatim report, Petrograd, 1921, p. 20.

this direction was the granting of concessions to foreign capitalists without whose help the economic reconstruction of Russia was unthinkable. A mere importation of technical equipment and machinery from abroad, he maintained, was no solution of the problem. Under existing conditions, Russia was incapable of using foreign machinery efficiently. The only way out of the present difficulties was to turn over certain of the national resources to the control of foreign capitalists and experts under the supervision of the Soviet Government. Any other course would immediately retard the economic recovery of the country.[8]

Kamenev, in a detailed report on "The Soviet Republic in a Capitalist Environment," struck a similar note. He pointed out the necessity of an intelligent and sober attitude toward relations between the Soviet Union and the capitalist world at a time when the anticipated help from western Europe in the shape of a revolution in at least one or two capitalist countries was not forthcoming. Had such a revolution taken place, the whole problem from the Soviet point of view would have been immensely simplified and the question of international agreement, loans, and concessions would not have arisen at all. While hoping for such a development, it was imperative that the Union should be in position to deal with the situation as it existed at the present time, and to struggle for the existence of an isolated socialist republic. The attempts of Moscow to reach an un-

[8] *Ibid.*, p. 21.

derstanding with the capitalist countries did not mean, of course, the abandonment of the ultimate aims of the Soviets. Agreements with the capitalists "are merely a new form of the struggle—the struggle for the consolidation of communism in one of the isolated countries. We never thought of establishing communism in one isolated country. We have found ourselves in a position, however, which necessitates our retaining the fundamentals of the communist system, the fundamentals of the socialist state, the Soviet proletarian republic, encircled by capitalist nations." [9] Whether this was a feasible task was, in the opinion of Kamenev, an idle and academic question. The urgent problem was how to maintain the Soviet rule in Russia until the proletariat of some other country should come to its rescue. The criticism advanced by some of the members of the Communist Party, that the participation of the Soviet Union in the economic intercourse with the capitalist world would necessarily lead to the strengthening of capitalism by supplying it with labor and raw materials, was dismissed by Kamenev as distinctly petty bourgeois. The disintegration of world capitalism, he argued, had reached so advanced a stage that the use of Russian raw materials could not retard the revolutionary processes in Europe even for a day. On the other hand, the development of the productive forces of the world economy did not hinder the progress of the proletarian revolution, but on the contrary stimulated it by intensifying the contradic-

[9] *Ibid.*, pp. 176–182.

tions of the capitalist world. Turning to the question
of foreign concessions, Kamenev declared that although the economic reconstruction of Russia was
possible even without foreign capital at the price
of terrible and heroic sacrifices on the part of Russian workers, it would be so slow that the Union
could never keep pace with the progress of other
countries, handicapped as they were by capitalist
methods. In order to reach the ultimate aim of communism the participation of capitalism in the reconstruction of Russia was therefore imperative.[10]

The ideas of Lenin and Kamenev were embodied
in the resolutions adopted by the tenth congress of
the Party. After paying homage to the heroic spirit
displayed by the Russian proletariat in its struggle
against the White armies and its backers, one of the
resolutions declared that this victory and the failure
of foreign intervention, coupled with the desire of
the capitalist nations to increase their profits by
exploiting Russia's natural resources, had created a
situation favorable for the resumption of economic
and political relations between the Soviet Union and
the capitalist world. It should be used, the resolution said, "primarily for the development of the
productive forces of the republic, and the better-
ment of the position of the working class. This fundamental . . . problem could not be solved on a
large scale and within a short time without making
use of foreign technique, and the implements of
production manufactured abroad." The resolution

[10] *Ibid.*, pp. 176–182.

accordingly endorsed the policy of foreign concessions on which the Soviet government had already
embarked.[11]

The practical value of these declarations was
greatly enhanced by the fact that in the course of
the same month, March, 1921, the Moscow government signed a trade agreement with Great Britain,
the first of its kind. The keen sense of political and
economic realities which is so much in the tradition
of British statesmanship and diplomacy, and which
had so often brought upon the government at London undeserved accusations of selfishness and treachery, had once more showed the road which was soon
to be followed by other nations. Before the end of
the year the Soviet Union had resumed trade relations with a number of European countries.

THE THIRD CONGRESS OF THE COMINTERN

It became the duty of the third congress of the
Communist International, which was in session from
June 22 to July 12, 1921, to determine its attitude
toward the new situation which had developed since
the second congress of 1920. The third congress met
in a much more sober atmosphere than either of its
predecessors. This was admitted a little later even
by Zinoviev.[12] In his inaugural address, the President of the Third International reviewed the development of the world revolutionary movement

[11] *Ibid.*, pp. 186–187.
[12] *Odinnadtsati Sezd Rossiskoi Kommunisticheskoi Partii*
(Eleventh Congress of the Russian Communist Party), March 22–
April 2, 1922, verbatim report, Moscow, 1922, p. 188.

since the second congress. It was not a very encouraging picture. The revolutionary outbursts in Italy accompanied by the seizure of factories by the workmen and by attempts to organize a Red army had ended in a failure, the responsibility for which was laid at the door of the labor leaders, who had betrayed the movement to its class enemies. A strong revolutionary movement of the Czechoslovak proletariat in December, 1920, had been no more successful. A similar fate had befallen the labor disturbance in Germany in the spring of 1921. Side by side with these more important outbreaks, a number of smaller manifestations of the revolutionary spirit had taken place in other countries. While conceding the defeat of each individual movement, Zinoviev refused to agree with those enemies of communism who saw in this lack of success the defeat of the policy of the Comintern. On the contrary, he maintained, they had been most useful experiences in which the young communist parties had been learning their trade, and had been discovering how to avoid in the future the mistakes they had committed in the past. The whole history of the world proletariat consisted of such defeats.[18]

The list of revolutionary outbreaks given by Zinoviev was amplified by Trotsky, who added to it the strike of British miners and the general strike in Norway, both of which took place in 1921. While describing them as "important factors in the great

---

[18] G. Zinoviev's address at the opening of the third congress of the Third International, in *Kommunisticheski Internatsional*, No. 18, 1921, pp. 4480–4482.

struggle," Trotsky rightly remarked that their most significant result was that the bourgeoisie still remained in power. He agreed with Zinoviev that the failure of the labor outbursts to achieve their ultimate purpose should in no wise be interpreted as the bankruptcy of the Third International. Its general principles remained unshaken, but their practical application must be brought in line with the new conditions. "What we have to face now," said Trotsky, "is not the elementary and chaotic rush forward, the first stage of which we saw in Europe in 1918–1919. We believed then—and with a certain historical justification—that during the disorganization of the bourgeoisie this rush forward might go on in continuously increasing waves, that in this process the intelligence of the leading groups of the proletariat would be awakened, and that in this manner the proletariat would assume the control of the government within one or two years. Such an historical possibility did exist, but it failed to materialize. History has granted the bourgeoisie . . . a fairly long breathing space." [14]

There was nothing particularly surprising about it, argued Trotsky. The bourgeoisie had merely displayed a greater ability to adapt itself to post-war conditions of impoverishment than it had been credited with. The general situation was somewhat more complex than it had formerly been; but it was still favorable. Revolution was not as manageable as

[14] *Treti Vsemirni Kongress Kommunisticheskago Internatsionala (Third World Congress of the Communist International),* verbatim report, Petrograd, 1922, p. 44.

was originally imagined. It followed its own course, had its own crises, its own ups and downs. The situation in 1921 was very different from what it was at the time of the first and the second congress. "Then," he said, "we took a broad view, we were satisfied with determining the basic line of our policy, and we said to ourselves: 'Let us follow this road because around this banner we shall rally the proletariat and conquer the world.' . . . Taken as a whole, our line is still valid. We have only failed in the past to foresee its deviations and fluctuations, but now we are conscious of them. . . . Only now we begin to see and understand that we are not yet on the threshold of one realization of our ultimate aim —the seizing of power on a world scale, the world revolution. Then—in 1919—we said that it was a question of months; we say now that it is a question of years. We do not know exactly how long it will take, but we know that we are moving toward that goal and that our position to-day is much stronger than it used to be. . . . The struggle will be, perhaps, a long one and our progress will be slower than we desire. It will be a difficult struggle, one that will require many sacrifices. But we are learning from experience. . . . We were ready, and we shall be ready in the future, to use every situation, whatever it may be, for the revolutionary offensive and for the conquest of political power." [15]

This new attitude of the leaders of the Comintern called for a new program of practical policies. It was

[15] *Ibid.*, pp. 45–46.

provided in the report on the tactics of the Third International submitted by Karl Radek. The Comintern, he argued, will continue to exist even if world revolution suffers a defeat. But if capitalist society is granted a long breathing space, the activities of the Comintern will be different from what they are during a period of increasing revolutionary activities. In the former case they will no longer consist in preparing the working classes to deal with any possible emergency during a civil war, but in organization and agitation, in forming detachments for the remote struggle of the future. Radek strongly emphasized his belief that there was no reason to expect that any improvement would take place in the economic position of the capitalist world, but it was the duty of the Comintern to be ready to face any new situation. Its general policy, therefore, was to be based on the assumption that the forces of world revolution would continue to grow and that they would unite for new struggles. The delays in the coming of world revolution, he maintained, were anticipated in the Russian communist press as early as 1918, when it became clear that the revolutionary parties headed by the Comintern were to face a protracted struggle and must be ready to accept occasional defeats. The present period was not a period of transition from open attack to trench warfare, but that of the formation of the great armies of the world proletariat. The chief problem with which the leaders of the revolution were confronted in the present was the winning over of the masses to the cause of communism. "The most important question we have to settle," said Radek, "is this: How can the communist parties exercise influence upon the spontaneous movements of the proletariat, unite them, intensify them and turn them into a struggle for power? This most important question can be settled only through the study of the activities of our movement, of what we experienced in our greatest conflicts, and by letting all that teach us our most useful lesson." [16]

After surveying the recent labor disturbances in different quarters of the world, Radek admitted that the proletariat had suffered a defeat; but this was a defeat of local movements, not of the proletarian revolution as such. It was only now that it had really begun to grow. To accelerate and organize its growth the Comintern must have a fully developed program of action. Radek agreed with Trotsky that the revolution in its development did not follow a straight line, and that while it continually advanced it had its rises and falls. This did not mean that the leaders of the revolution must remain idle. Revolutionary propaganda and revolutionary action were not mutually exclusive, as was sometimes suggested. On the contrary, real revolutionary propaganda was the best preparation for action. "If only, because we are approaching a time of hard battles," Radek exhorted, "I must tell you this, comrades: You must be the mighty alarm bell which calls to the struggle; now we are merely a tiny little bell. If we are to-

[16] *Ibid.*, pp. 204–210.

day members of the great Communist International, it is not because we, the International, have carried on a successful agitation, but because the Russian proletariat and the Russian Red army have agitated and successfully, by suffering hunger and giving their blood, because this struggle, because this Russian revolution has played the part of the mighty alarm bell of the Communist International. Our propaganda work is everywhere still in its preliminary stage, it has not yet succeeded in reaching the masses. If we realize that we are on the eve of heavy fighting we must say to ourselves: 'First of all, and by all possible methods—nearer to the masses!' Then, next, we must say to ourselves: 'For the very reason that we do not know what to-morrow has in store for us, for the very reason that to-morrow we may be drawn into the mighty struggle, we must get ready for it!' A revolution cannot be organized. One can command an army, but not a revolution. It is an unruly, an elementary movement, and it determines our method of action; and that is to make clear to the political consciousness of the masses the meaning of the struggle, and to organize and coördinate the 'shock' detachments of the proletariat, its vanguard, so that it can, on the crest of the revolutionary wave, dash forward and lead the masses in the struggle." Preliminary organization work and direct action could exist side by side. The real enemy of organization was inaction. Every situation must be met by the methods it required. "Revolutionary agitation is struggle, revolutionary

propaganda is struggle, and so are underground organizations, the military training of the proletariat,
party schools, demonstrations, uprisings. From every situation, the maximum result. That must be
our slogan." Premature action, however, was quite
as harmful as opportunism. Psychologically, both
were the offspring of impatience. And Radek closed
his address with this advice: "Do not ask of to-day
what belongs to to-morrow." [17]

The question of revolutionary tactics very largely
dominated the debates of the congress. Lenin's report was devoted to the tactics to be followed by the
Russian Communist Party. "When in due course
we entered the world revolution," he said, "we did
not do this because we believed that we might
change its course, but because a number of conditions seemed to necessitate such action. Our argument was this: either the world revolution would
come to our assistance, and then our victory would
be certain, or we should do our modest revolutionary
work conscious that even our defeat would serve
the cause of the revolution. It was clear to us that
without the support of the international world revolution, the victory of the proletarian revolution
could not be achieved. Even before the [Russian]
revolution, as well as after it, we expected that either
then, or at least very soon, revolution would take
place in other countries where capitalist development had reached a more advanced stage; or, in
the contrary case, that we would perish. In spite

[17] *Ibid.*, pp. 225–227.

of this belief and under the most adverse conditions we did all in our power to safeguard the Soviet system because we knew that we were working not merely for ourselves, but also for the world revolution. . . . The actual trend of revolutionary development differed somewhat from our expectations. Up to now we have had no revolution in the other great and more advanced capitalist countries. It is true that the revolution is making progress . . . and this is the real reason why the international bourgeoisie, although economically and militarily a hundred times stronger than we are, is unable to strangle us. . . . What are we to do now? We must undertake a careful study of how to prepare revolution and its actual development in the advanced capitalist countries." [18]

In the discussion that followed, Radek, replying to the criticism of a German delegate that the interests and policies of the Soviet Union were sometimes in conflict with those of the proletariat of other European countries, made a strong plea for Russia's part in the world revolutionary movement. "We are now," he said, "in the transition stage from foreign war to internal peace, and economic problems are acquiring a fundamental importance. . . . If you do not deny that Russia has been so far the stronghold of the world revolution . . . then you will be forced to recognize that all that we have done so far is essential from the point of view of the world revolution. . . . The reasons for the policies of Soviet

[18] *Ibid.*, pp. 354–355.

Russia are perfectly clear. They are the necessary consequence not only of the situation which exists in Russia, but also of the situation in which the proletariat of the world finds itself. If the question is asked whether this policy is not fraught with danger, the answer is that it unquestionably is. Lenin has stated in his thesis that an isolated, proletarian government can continue to exist only during a limited period of time. At our meetings we have discussed this danger at length. There is only one real cure for this situation, the acceleration of the world revolution." [19]

Bukharin, the eminent authority on communist theory, took a similar view. "Shall we survive or not? It is at present impossible to give a definite answer to this question. The important thing for us at present is to gain time. If we are lost, this does not mean that the revolution in western European countries is also lost. You will profit by our experience. But, at any rate, we are not yet lost." [20]

The ideas which dominated the third congress of the Comintern found their official expression in the resolutions it passed, which laid down the principles on which the policies of the communist parties were to be based in the future. The most important among them was the new slogan, "To the masses!" Translated from abstract into concrete terms it meant the participation of communist organizations

[19] *Ibid.*, pp. 365–366.
[20] *Ibid.*, p. 382.

in the everyday petty struggle of the working class, even for the most insignificant improvements of its position; the participation in all workers' organizations from the Soviets down to athletic and musical clubs; the untiring propaganda of the ideas of proletarian dictatorship in all of them; the winning over of the proletariat to the cause of communism; the stubborn, tenacious, and systematic preparation of the masses for the approaching battles; the most careful work in the formation of underground revolutionary organizations; the patient and painstaking labor of providing the workers with arms; the creation of powerful and independent communist parties free from all outside elements. The gaining over of trade unions to communism.

The second important conclusion reached by the congress was the recognition of the fact that it was idle to expect that a small minority of communists, not yet enjoying the whole-hearted support of the masses of labor, might at any time, and by some daring outbreak, win a victory over the bourgeoisie in an open armed struggle. It rejected the idea advocated by its extreme members that an "activization" of the labor movement could be achieved by the simple expedient of applying high-handed methods to it. This did not mean, of course, that the activities of the communist parties were to be limited to propaganda. It was still their duty to assume the lead in any labor disturbances, but they were to refrain from decisive revolutionary action—from armed uprising—unless they were reasonably sure that the general situation was favorable to the successful issue of the struggle. This newly acquired wisdom was the result of the severe disappointments which the Comintern had experienced in the course of the preceding years. The situation immediately following the war, it was maintained, was exceptionally propitious to the immediate overthrow of capitalism. If in spite of this the world revolution failed to materialize, this was due to the lack of organization among the workers and the treason of labor leaders who went over into the camp of the bourgeoisie. The history of the labor movement in Italy in 1919 and early 1920 offered a particularly instructive, if highly regrettable, example of such treason. The strengthening of the revolutionary organization and the weeding out of pseudo-communists among the leaders was therefore the foremost and immediate task.

These decisions of the third congress were naturally severely criticized by the more uncompromising and impatient members of the Comintern, who denounced them as a flagrant surrender to the bourgeoisie and the abandonment of the great aim of the revolutionary proletariat—the world revolution. Martov, for instance, spoke openly of "the twilight of the Comintern." And it is highly indicative of the long road the Third International had travelled since 1919 that it was Zinoviev who now passionately defended its new policy and interpreted it as a striking victory over the bourgeoisie, who were thus given irrefutable proof that communists were not dreamers and fools, but enemies who were earnest, resolute, intelligent, and willing to make necessary concessions to assure the final triumph of their cause. While applauding the wise policy of the Comintern and recognizing that the revolutionary tide was at low ebb, Zinoviev could not, naturally, altogether renounce his attitude of two years before, that of hoping against hope. "Not being a prophet," he wrote, "none of us can predict with exactitude how many months or years will elapse before we shall behold the proletariat triumph in the first of those important countries upon which actually depends the fate of the world revolution. But there is one thing we are all sure of, and a survey of economic conditions in Europe at the third congress has proved it again: the revolution is not over; the time is not distant when new battles will take place. And they will shake Europe and the whole world with a violence greater than all former battles put together." [21]

THE BEGINNING OF THE NEW ERA

The recognition of the idea that the world revolution was not just around the corner but would, perhaps, have to be given a very long time to ripen its fruit, continued to gain ground in the years following the third congress of the Comintern. The corollaries necessary to its acceptance were, first, a policy directed to the strengthening of the communist parties in the various countries as laid down by the

[21] G. Zinoviev, *Taktika Kominterna (Tactics of the Comintern),* in *Kommunisticheski Internatsional,* 1921, No. 18, pp. 4459–4477.

third congress, and, second, persistent attempts to resume normal trade relations with the rest of the world. And as time went on and the Soviet rulers had to come to grips with the grim necessities of an extremely complicated domestic and international situation, their attention became gradually more and more centered upon the Soviet Union as something that was no longer a mere starting point in that world revolution on whose success or failure the ultimate fate of the Soviet experiment depended, but as in itself an aim of primary importance, not only from the national point of view but also from that of the proletariat of the world. This idea did not triumph at once, but made converts through the slow and painful process of party discussions and cleavages until it emerged in the finished form of Stalin's doctrine of "Socialism in a single country" in the autumn of 1924. It was during this period that the close interdependence between Soviet domestic and foreign policy received official recognition, and the problem of the economic reconstruction of the country with the help of the capitalist nations was brought to the fore. In this connection the policy of concessions to foreign capital was given much prominence, it being assumed in those days that foreign capital was an essential element in putting Russia economically on its feet, a point of view which has been abandoned since.

We have already seen that the Soviet Union resumed trade relation with a number of European countries in the course of 1921. In April–May, 1922, it made its first appearance at an important international conference, that of Genoa. The new spirit which animated the Soviet Government was clearly stated in this connection by Lenin. "The most burning political problem of the day is Genoa," he said. ". . . Naturally, we are going to Genoa not as communists, but as merchants. We want to trade and they want to trade. We want to make profits and they want to make profits. The issue of the struggle will depend, although in a small degree, on the skill of our diplomats." [22] The outlook for the Genoa conference, it is well known, was never too bright. It was further complicated by the bombshell of the Rapallo Treaty signed by Germany and the Soviet representatives. In spite of Lenin's conciliatory remarks, the general attitude of the Soviet delegation was such as to make the reaching of an understanding between them and the European Powers all but impossible. Genoa failed to accomplish its purpose and a new conference met at The Hague in June of the same year, but with no more success.

The Soviet Government was again represented at the Lausanne conference called in September, 1922, to settle the Turkish problem. Its deliberations ended in a deadlock in January, 1923, but were resumed later. On this occasion the Soviet Government showed a greater desire to collaborate, and, in July, 1923, finally signed a convention providing for

[22] *Odinnadtsati Sezd Rossiskoi Kommunisticheskoi Partii Bolshevikov (Eleventh Congress of the Russian Communist Bolshevik Party)*, 22 March–2 April, 1922, verbatim report, Moscow, 1922, pp. 7–8.

the demilitarization of the Dardanelles, although its provisions were not precisely gratifying to Moscow.

While the Soviet Government was making a definite bid for official recognition by the capitalist nations and was seeking to develop its trade relations with the outside world, the Communist Party and other organizations affiliated with the Communist International were proceeding to develop the program of international revolutionary action along the lines laid down by the third congress. This policy, it will be remembered, was summarized in the slogan: "To the masses!" The work of putting it into practice was carried on under the general supervision of the Executive Committee of the Communist International by the various national communist parties and by the Profintern, or Red Labor International. The latter is an organization of trade unions which was devised as a method of bringing the organized labor movement within the influence of the communist parties. Its inaugural congress met in July, 1921, and its immediate purpose was stated as that of counteracting the influence of the "yellow" Amsterdam International, a non-communist international labor organization. It was between the third and the fourth congress of the Comintern that the so-called "tactics of the united labor front" came into existence. This rather involved formula was used to describe a policy which had for its purpose the uniting of the efforts of all workers willing to fight against capitalism, even those who did not embrace the communist creed. Such were, for instance, the syndicalists and the anarchists. By including them in the organizations fighting capitalism it was hoped not only to increase the influence of the communist parties and of the Comintern, but also to free the labor movement from those pernicious labor leaders who preferred compromise with the bourgeoisie to class struggle. It was also during this period that it became customary to identify communism with international peace, and to emphasize war as the inescapable consequence of the capitalist system.

The fourth congress of the Comintern, which was in session from November 5 to December 3, 1922, further elaborated the policies announced by its predecessor and emphasized the importance of that united front of labor which was to find its fullest expression in the establishment of governments of workers. It was highly characteristic of the general spirit of the time that Lenin's report, *Five Years of the Russian Revolution and the Outlook for the World Revolution,* was largely devoted to the defense of the New Economic Policy. And it contained some illuminating remarks on the necessity of making provisions for a retreat. "I personally think," he said, "that it would be better if, on their first reading, we discussed all our programs only provisionally, then had them printed, and did not now this year come to a final decision. Why? First of all, of course, because we have hardly had time enough carefully to discuss them. And also because we have given practically no consideration to the

possibility of a retreat and how it should be safe-
guarded. Now this is a question which must be
taken into account in rebuilding the world, abolishing capitalism and the resulting difficult conditions
under which the socialist system must be set up. To
plan what we shall do if we decide on a frontal attack and then win a victory is not enough. Under
revolutionary conditions this is not so difficult, nor
is it so important. At least this is not the most important thing. During a revolution there are moments when the enemy loses his head; and if we
fall upon him at the right time we can win an
easy victory. But this in itself does not mean anything, because our enemy, if he has sufficient self-
control, may already have mobilized his forces, and
the like. He may provoke our attack and then throw
us back for many years. This is why I think that
the idea that we must prepare for the possibility of
a retreat is of extreme importance; and it is essential not merely as a matter of theory, but also of
practical politics, that this question should be carefully examined by all those elements which are getting ready to launch an attack against capitalism in
the near future. They should consider how to cover
their retreat." [23]

Similar ideas were advanced by the other leaders
of the Comintern. Trotsky defended the New Economic Policy on the ground that political power in

[23] *Chetverti Vsemirni Kongress Kommunisticheskago Internatsionala (Fourth World Congress of the Communist Internatsional)*, November 5–December 3, 1922, selected reports,
speeches, and resolutions, Moscow—Petrograd, 1923, pp. 62–64.

Russia was now in the hands of the working class. Any revival of the capitalist forms of production and exchange was of no importance so long as this fundamental condition was maintained.[24]

Radek, in a report on the advance of capital, pleaded for a better organization of the communist parties and their leader, the Comintern. He pointed out that a striking change had taken place in the attitude of the working classes toward the world revolution between 1919 and 1920. During the earlier period, socialism was gaining all along the line, and the difference between the communists and the non-party labor was not one of aim, but of method. "On the contrary, in the case of the present period," Radek sadly remarked, "in spite of the fact that the crisis of the world proletariat is by no means over, the characteristic feature is the loss of faith by the proletariat in the possibility of seizing power in the near future. It is now on the defensive." [25] The proletariat must learn that the only road to the overthrow of capitalism is civil war. There is no other way. The organization of the masses of labor is therefore of primary importance. In this respect a great deal still remains to be done. "It is highly indicative of the general position of the labor movement," he said, "that our communist agitation, even in the countries where our parties are particularly well organized, has still an abstract character, that it is not imbued with the passionate conviction of

[24] *Ibid.*, pp. 109 *sqq.*
[25] *Ibid.*, p. 132.

men who are convinced that they are fighting for aims which are actually attainable in the near future. Our struggle still gives the impression of being pure agitation; and if we do not want to see our debates die from low blood pressure, and our congresses acquire the semblance of party clubs engrossed in theoretical discussions of tendencies of development, then our parties must adopt in practice a policy different from the one they have pursued so far, one not differing merely from the point of view of general political trend and direction, but in aggressive spirit." [26] The future of the world revolution depended very largely on the work of the communist parties and of the Comintern. "The communists form the vanguard of the working class. They believe in the dictatorship of the proletariat. But the non-partisan rank and file of labor will remain outside the struggle unless forced to take part in it by circumstances. At the present time the majority of the working class has no thought of seizing political power, that is clear." [27] This pessimistic conclusion was quite in keeping with the general tone of the debate.

NEW DISAPPOINTMENTS AND NEW HOPES

The eighteen months which elapsed between the fourth and the fifth congress of the Comintern were a period fertile in hopes, disappointments, and real achievements in both domestic and foreign policies.

[26] *Ibid.*, pp. 140–141.
[27] *Ibid.*, p. 172.

A great revival of revolutionary activities took place in Moscow in 1923 in connection with the disorganization in Germany brought about by the occupation of the Ruhr. It was confidently believed at the time by an influential section of the Russian Communist Party that communism would triumph in Germany in the very near future. These hopes failed to materialize. The death of Lenin deprived Bolshevism of its recognized leader, and was followed by a stubborn struggle for leadership from which Stalin emerged the victor. The political future of a number of the leaders of the Comintern was extremely uncertain. Among them were some outstanding personalities such as Trotsky, Zinoviev, and Bukharin. On the other hand, the New Economic Policy brought a marked improvement in the economic situation; and economic questions of reorganization and industrialization were rapidly taking precedence over purely political problems in the minds of the new rulers of the Soviet Union. In February, 1924, Russia obtained de jure recognition by the British Government and by Italy; and in October, by France. Russian foreign relations were still subject to grave and frequent disturbances, among which the raid on the Soviet Trade Delegation in Berlin in May, 1924, and the "Zinoviev letter," which played so important a part in the British elections of the same year, attracted particular attention. The extreme care taken by the Soviet Government to deny the accusations made against it in connection with the "Zinoviev letter," which contained nothing that had not been proclaimed previously and openly on innumerable earlier occasions by the Comintern, was in itself a striking revelation of the new attitude of Moscow. The struggle for the overthrow of capitalism was still, of course, an important item in the Soviet program, but it was no longer quite as important as in the first years of the régime. It may be no exaggeration to say that the Comintern itself began to lose some of its former influence in high Soviet circles.

In this new situation the general attitude of the Soviet Government and of the Comintern toward world problems obviously needed revision. The necessity of a *rapprochement* with the capitalist countries was now admitted even by Zinoviev. In an address delivered in the spring of 1923, he declared that the trend of Russia's foreign policy was toward a better understanding and closer coöperation with the exploited nations of the East and with Germany after her defeat. But this did not preclude a *rapprochement* with the Entente Powers, even with France, though she was then engaged in the occupation of the Ruhr, because there was no doubt that the majority of the French people were in sympathy with communism. This was also true of the relations of the Soviet Union with England, Japan, and the United States.[28]

Zinoviev then proceeded to develop the theory of

[28] *Dvenadtsati Sezd Rossiskoi Kommunisticheskoi Partii Bolshevikov (Twelfth Congress of the Russian Communist Bolshevik Party)*, 17–25 April, 1923, verbatim report, Moscow, 1923, pp. 12–14.

the close interdependence of domestic and foreign policy which, in the case of Soviet Russia, at least, seems to have been well justified. "It is not so easy to draw a mechanical distinction between foreign and domestic policy," he said. "It is wrong to imagine that foreign policy rests on one plate, and domestic policy on another. A shrewd German statesman who has published a book on the inter-relationship of foreign and domestic policies has given the following formula: *Die innere Politik denkt, die aüssere lenkt.* That is, domestic policy plans, and foreign policy has the final decision. By this I mean to say that there is the closest interdependence between the two. This applies to the Soviet state and to Soviet politics. Our domestic policy is closely and inseparably bound up with our foreign policy." [29] The congress of the Communist Party accordingly passed a resolution in which it fully endorsed the policy of the government in maintaining its monopoly of foreign trade and in encouraging foreign capitalists to invest their money in the development of the natural resources of the country. [30]

Similar views were advanced by Zinoviev a year later, in May, 1924, at the thirteenth congress of the Communist Party. "We must particularly remember to-day," he said, "that never before was our international policy so closely bound up with our domestic policy as it is now. And this is why. In the very near future we shall have to decide the

[29] *Ibid.*, p. 189.
[30] *Ibid.*, p. 617.

following questions: whether we shall or shall not
pay the loans; whether we shall or shall not pay
anything on account as interest; whether we shall
or shall not make concessions in the matter of the
monopoly of foreign trade; and how much grain we
shall export. All these questions form a most important part not only of our foreign but also of our
domestic policy." And to emphasize his point, Zinoviev enumerated the four elements which, in his
opinion, determined at the time the foreign policy
of the Soviet Union. They were: (1) the growth of
the international labor movement, the proletarian
struggle under the leadership of the Comintern; (2)
foreign policy in the narrow sense of the term; (3)
the question of foreign concessions; and (4) the
monopoly of foreign trade and the connected problem of the export of Russian grain.[31] This attitude
again received the full support of the congress in an
appropriate resolution.[32] Although the Communist
Party was still sticking to its old revolutionary
phraseology, the inescapable conclusion from reading the proceedings of the congress is that domestic
preoccupations were getting the upper hand over
problems of purely international politics.

THE FIFTH CONGRESS OF THE COMINTERN

The fifth congress of the Comintern which met
from June 17 to July 8, 1924, put the stamp of of-

[31] *Trinadtsati Sezd Rossiskoi Kommunisticheskoi Partii Bol-
sheviko (Thirteenth Congress of the Russian Communist Bolshevik Party)*, 23–31 May, 1924, verbatim report, Moscow, 1924,
p. 50.
[32] *Ibid.*, p. 634.

ficial recognition upon the now generally accepted fact that the "heroic" period of the proletarian revolution had been, temporarily at least, brought to an end. It was fitting that the proclamation of the approaching new era in the Comintern's work should come from its fiery and eloquent president, Zinoviev. A few weeks earlier, at the thirteenth congress of the Russian Communist Party, he had already confessed that he had learned much since 1919. "Taken as a whole," he said, defending the policies of the Comintern, "we have given a correct analysis of the objective tendencies of world development. But our evaluation of the factor 'time' has not been altogether justified. This is perfectly clear to us to-day. There was a time—during the peace negotiations of Brest-Litovsk—when even Vladimir Ilich [Lenin] believed that the victory of revolution in a number of advanced European countries was a question of merely two or three months. There was a time when we, in the Central Committee of the Party, measured in hours the progress of events in Germany and Austria. In this sense we, of course, made a mistake. But fortunately for us, comrades, we have misjudged the possibilities of the factor 'time' in two directions. We have misjudged them not only in the sense of the probable advent of revolution, but also in the sense of the chance of its retreat. First, then, we believed that if we seized governmental power we should by this very fact *to-morrow* give free hand to revolution in other countries. Second, we believed that if this by any chance did not take place, then we, as an isolated revolution, as a sole revolutionary country left to itself, could not survive and were doomed to destruction. . . . We were not unlike an inexperienced army which had never been under fire, a wholly new army made up solely of fresh recruits, who had never fought a battle and were familiar, therefore, with neither the rules of attack nor retreat. We did not understand the laws of space and time. Now we have gained a certain experience. The events have taken such a turn that the question of world revolution is not a question of three months, but of a much longer period; but the events have also taken such a turn that the first presumably isolated revolution has survived much longer than we used to think it possible. This is why we now face the future in a much more realistic manner than we did in the past." And Zinoviev proceeded to argue that the Russian revolution was, in fact, not isolated at all because it had powerful allies in the proletariat of the bourgeois countries.[33]

In his inaugural address to the fifth congress of the Comintern Zinoviev expressed similar views. He reviewed the course of the revolutionary movement since 1919 and charged the labor leaders with treachery which had kept the world revolution from materializing.[34] And in his report, *Tactics of the Executive Committee of the Comintern,* he also admitted that in the course of the first years of their

[33] Verbatim report of the thirteenth congress of the Russian Communist Party, p. 42.

[34] *Pyati Vsemirni Kongress Kommunisticheskago Internatsionala (Fifth World Congress of the Communist International),* June 17–July 8, 1924, verbatim report, Moscow—Leningrad, 1925, Vol. I, pp. 9 *sqq.*

existence the communist parties in most countries were nothing but societies for propaganda. The spontaneous movements of the masses, exhausted by the war, were wrongly interpreted as a genuine shift toward communism. In fact it was merely an "optical illusion." [35] Pleading for a strengthening of the communist parties, Zinoviev agreed with some of his critics that the death of Lenin was an irreparable blow to the cause of communism. Not only the confidence of the masses but even the confidence of the leaders themselves in the soundness of their policies was badly shaken when their decisions could no longer be checked by Lenin's unfailing revolutionary foresight. [36] Zinoviev ended the discussion with what for him was a note of deep pessimism. "It would have been easy for the third congress to produce a paper scheme proving that in the next year or two we would witness the complete breakdown of capitalism. But what would be the use of such a scheme if it had no relation to the facts? We have learned much in the course of the last years. We have come to understand, among other things, that the term 'breakdown of capitalism' must be used with caution. The breakdown of capitalism is indeed inevitable. Capitalism is doomed. But we must see things in their true light and must estimate the factor of 'time' with greater caution than in the past." [37] Zinoviev had, indeed, travelled a long way from his original position in 1919!

[35] *Ibid.*, pp. 45–46.
[36] *Ibid.*, p. 88.
[37] *Ibid.*, p. 438.

It would, of course, be entirely wrong to imagine that disappointment with the immediate revolutionary outlook implied anything like the abandonment of the struggle. On the contrary, it was to continue, although by somewhat different methods which we shall discuss in a moment. But no revolutionary movement can live long on promises relating to a rather distant future, however enchanting such remote perspectives. More tangible, concrete, and accessible aims are needed and these were found in the establishing of the Soviet Union itself. This was a field which offered practically no limit to the enthusiasm, energy, and initiative of a young and vigorous nation. Domestic policy was, as we have seen, taking an ever increasing place in the preoccupations of the Soviet leaders. It soon became one of the tasks of the Soviet writers to prove to themselves and the outside world that whatever was done in Russia was done not so much for selfish or national considerations, but for those of the world proletariat. It is from this point of view that at the fifth congress of the Comintern Bukharin undertook the defense of the New Economic Policy. The latter, it will be remembered, was inaugurated by Lenin in the spring of 1921, and consisted in restoring the market which had been completely destroyed under War Communism in 1918–1920, and in allowing a certain limited amount of freedom to private capital and private initiative. This policy was, naturally, much criticized by the more orthodox communists, who saw in it a shameful surrender to capitalism.

Bukharin pointed out in his report to the congress that it was customary even among the responsible Soviet leaders to apologize for the New Economic Policy and to consider it merely as a measure of political expediency, as a timely concession to petty bourgeois elements. This attitude had completely changed since, he said, and the New Economic Policy appeared to-day as one which was fully justified on general grounds, leaving wholly aside the question of expediency. According to his theory, under the New Economic Policy the great state-controlled enterprises were waging a struggle against the small private producers through the machinery of market competition. On the surface the situation was similar to that which prevailed in a capitalist society; but there was a fundamental difference. The difference was that in the Soviet Union the great enterprises were owned by the state; that is, by the proletariat. Therefore, Bukharin declared, the competition between such great enterprises belonging to the proletariat (that is, which were state owned) and those that were small and privately owned was really a revolutionary struggle, a class struggle against the bourgeoisie. "Such a prosaic thing as market competition is nothing but a new and specialized form of class struggle." And as such it was a contribution to the revolutionary arsenal of the world.[38]

In its resolutions, the fifth congress analyzed the world situation and arrived at the conclusion that

[38] *Ibid.*, pp. 496–500.

the "democratic-pacifist era" (the Labor Government in England, Herriot and the *Cartel des Gauches* in France) had really nothing to do with either democracy or peace. It was a mere camouflage to disguise the further progress of reaction. The antagonisms of the capitalistic world were growing more pronounced every day, and there was mad competition in armaments. These, of course, were statements which appeared in the resolutions of each of the congresses of the Comintern. The new orientation of the Comintern was stated in the following resolution: "The epoch of international revolution has begun. The tempo of its development in general and, in particular, the tempo of revolutionary progress on any given continent or in any given country cannot be forecast precisely. The entire situation is such that two courses are possible. (*a*) The slower and more protracted development of the proletarian revolution cannot be excluded; and (*b*) on the other hand the ground under capitalism is so undermined, and the contradictions of capitalism are developing so rapidly, that its breakdown in any given country may take place in the not distant future. The Comintern must so shape its policy as to be able to conform to either course. The flexibility of the policy of the Comintern must be such as to allow it to adapt itself to any new situation. And even should the development of events prove protracted, the Comintern must, as representing the great control and unchangeable body of the proletarian uprising, gather the masses about itself and prepare them for the revolutionary struggle for power." [39]

This practical task was to be carried out by the Comintern and it would do so by continuing to stress the slogan of the third congress: "To the masses!" To this was added a second task—the "bolshevization" of the sections of the Comintern; that is, of the national communist parties. By this was meant the reorganization of the communist parties in the various countries by using the experience of the Russian Communist Party. This process involved several general principles. The fundamentals of a truly Bolshevist party were stated to be as follows: (1) it should be a real mass party; that is, it should keep in closest touch with the masses of labor "and serve as the mouthpiece of their needs and hopes"; (2) it should be flexible; (3) it should be imbued with a revolutionary, Marxian spirit; (4) it should be centralized and prevent the formation of inside groups; (5) it should conduct propaganda in the bourgeois armies. [40] None of these demands were particularly new, except perhaps that they were now presented under the (to the communists) attractive name of "bolshevization." The congress also passed a resolution calling upon its followers to be ready for the coming battles against capitalism. These battles, however, as we have seen, did not in 1924 appear to be quite so near at hand as they had been in the past.

[39] *Ibid.*, Vol. II, p. 47.
[40] *Ibid.*, p. 47.

COMMUNISM VS. IMPERIALISTIC WARS

It is one of the commonplace doctrines of Marxian socialism that capitalism generates antagonisms between the classes, and that these antagonisms inevitably and necessarily lead to class war. Applying a similar analysis to the relations between the various nations, Lenin devised his theory of imperialism in accordance with which the antagonisms among the nations must continue to increase, and unavoidably lead to open, armed international struggles, of which the war of 1914–1918 was merely an early example. The inevitability of imperialistic wars was never seriously questioned in communist circles. As long as this was recognized and as long as it was believed that war was likely to bring in its trend the blessing of revolution, there was no special reason why the Soviet leaders should take any excessive interest in the problems of international peace. The experience of 1918–1920 had shown, however, that revolution, especially social revolution, does not necessarily follow a defeat in war. And as we have seen, the preservation of Russia as a centre of international communism gradually became one of the chief preoccupations of the Moscow leaders. The question of international wars appeared now in an entirely different light. Imperialistic wars were still believed to be a necessary consequence of the capitalistic system, but it became the duty of communism to postpone and delay them, to give the Soviet Union time to get a firm footing. Beginning with the second half of 1921, the denunciation of imperialistic wars became the subject of innumerable articles, books, speeches, and resolutions. For instance, in March, 1922, the Executive Committee of the Comintern, enlarged and sitting as a whole, passed a resolution which read in part: "The only effective method for preventing future wars is the proletarian revolution which overthrows capitalism, thereby makes possible economic reconstruction, and removes both class antagonisms and incompatibility between the interests of the various nations." And the resolution proceeded to lay down elaborate rules as to how class struggle for the prevention of international wars was to be conducted.[41] In April, 1923, Zinoviev discussed the question of Soviet policies in case of a new war, which he naturally declared to be unavoidable. What would be Russia's part in the approaching struggle? he asked. "I will be guilty of disclosing no important state secret," he said, answering his own question, "if I say that our strategy will be simple. We must be ready for the worst, for everything. But we must at the same time do all in our power to postpone the moment when we shall be forced to take an active part in the conflict. We need peace. So does our country. It is essential to the proletarian revolution that Russia should, economically, get upon her feet. Our strategy will therefore be simple. We shall put off joining the struggle as long as we can." [42] A similar view was expressed by Radek, who dwelt on the

[41] Lekhin, *Voina i Komintern (War the Comintern)*, in *Kommunisticheski Internatsional*, Nos. 5–6, 1924, pp. 66–67.

[42] Verbatim report of the twelfth congress of the Russian Communist Party, p. 13.

decisive part Russia would play in the coming struggle. He quoted the opinion of Lenin that for a world victory of the proletariat, the existence of the Soviet Union increased the chances by from 20 to 30 per cent. That this statement was in no way exaggerated would be made plain by an examination of the situation which would arise upon the outbreak of a new war. The geographical position of Russia, bordering as it did upon Germany in the west and upon British India in the east, immensely enhanced the potentialities of Russia as a decisive factor in the next international struggle. Her policy might be one of "wait and see" until the labor masses in the capitalistic countries had arisen, when she would swing to their side, and thus, by one stroke, gain the final victory for world revolution. Or Russia might ally herself with one of the belligerent parties, again in the interest of the international proletariat. The ruthless exploitation of the colonial peoples was likely to help Russia in forming a united front in the East against the oppressors. In the case of the countries of the West she would continue to use whatever instrument was best suited to break the chains of capitalism—whether the hammer or the file. "Capitalism is war. Those who wish to destroy war must destroy capitalism," Radek concluded.[43] Similar views were expressed over and over again in the years to come. But as the attention of the Soviet leaders became more and more engrossed in

[43] Karl Kadek, *Desyat let spustya (Ten Years Later)*, in *Kommunisticheski Internatsional*, Nos. 5–6, 1924, pp. 84–93.

domestic matters, the final and greater aim of abolishing war altogether through the destruction of capitalism grew dimmer, and the emphasis was put on the prevention of war in the immediate future as a necessary condition for the economic reconstruction of the country.

THE NEW DOGMA

Bolshevik theory, having its roots in the writings of an erudite German professor, has a marked leaning toward neat, well-ordered schemes of a distinct academic flavor. It was only too natural, therefore, that the change of attitude toward world revolution which we have been examining should find its expression in a dogmatic statement pleasing to the professorial mind. This statement came in a much advertised resolution dealing with the aims of the Comintern and the Russian Communist Party which was adopted by the fourteenth conference of the Russian Communist Party in April, 1925. The part of the resolution bearing particularly on the question in which we are now interested began with a quotation from Lenin that absolved him from all error in underestimating the time which the world revolution would actually take. "A revolution," Lenin wrote in 1915, "may consist, or, rather, will consist, of battles extending over many years, of several series of attacks followed by intermediate periods, the counter-revolutionary convulsions of the bourgeois system." This prophecy, the resolution declared, had been fully justified by the events of the past years. "One must distinguish," the resolution proceeded, "between: (*a*) a revolutionary situation, (*b*) an *immediate* revolutionary situation, and (*c*) an *outright* revolution." This was further supported by the following quotation from Lenin: "No Marxist will doubt that a revolution is impossible without a revolutionary situation, and that not every revolutionary situation leads to a revolution." The application of these ideas to reality was illustrated by examples. In Germany a revolutionary situation developed in 1914–1915. In 1917–1918 it grew into an immediate revolutionary situation; at the end of 1918 the latter became an outright revolution which degenerated into a mere bourgeois revolution. From 1920 to 1923 the immediate revolutionary situation gave place to a revolutionary situation. In 1923, Germany again developed an immediate revolutionary situation, which, however, failed to grow into a revolution. In 1925, Germany had again reverted to a mere revolutionary situation.

In Russia a definite revolutionary situation came into being in 1901–1902. In 1904–1905 it became an immediate revolutionary situation which culminated at the end of 1905 in outright revolution, which, however, was defeated. From 1906 to 1907 there continued to be an immediate revolutionary situation in Russia. From 1908 to 1915 there was a revolutionary situation, in spite of the "stabilization" of autocracy connected with the land reforms of Stolypin. In 1916 an immediate revolutionary situation was in evidence and in 1917 it culminated in the successful revolution which overthrew the monarchy.

A revolutionary situation was now (in 1925) beginning to show itself in Great Britain. But, admittedly, Great Britain was far from exhibiting an *immediate* revolutionary situation.

On a world scale, a revolutionary situation existed at the present time—that is, in 1925; and this was proved by the following argument: (*a*) the economic antagonisms which led to the war of 1914–1918 had not been eliminated, and could not be until a world proletarian revolution had taken place; (*b*) bourgeois Europe was pregnant with new imperialistic wars; (*c*) the East had awakened, and there, also, a revolutionary situation could be envisaged; (*d*) the first victorious proletarian revolution had consolidated itself within a territory which covered one-sixth of the surface of the globe; the very existence of the U. S. S. R. was a continuation of the process of the revolutionization of the world. It must be admitted, therefore, that a revolutionary situation was in existence in the world at large.[44]

There seems to be little doubt that this learned thesis, set forth in the best academic tradition, provided much mental relief for the Red professors and the more intellectual among the Soviet leaders. But it would readily be conceded that it was not exactly of a nature to set revolutionary enthusiasm aflame in

[44] *Chetirnadsataya Konferentsya Rossiskoi Kommunisticheskoi Partii Bolshevikov (Fourteenth Conference of the Russian Communist Bolshevik Party),* verbatim report, Moscow—Leningrad, 1925, pp. 306–308.

the masses of a nation, when most Russians could hardly read, and certainly would not be able to understand the erudite logic of the Communist Party. Something else more tangible, more concrete, and also more accessible to the imagination of the people was obviously needed. If the heroic spirit of early revolutionary days was to be revived, the country must be set an understandable and relatively simple task, and not asked to sit back and observe the mysterious and obscure shiftings of revolutionary situations, immediate revolutionary situations, and outright revolutions—a hazardous task in any case, as the Soviet leaders had learned only too well from their own bitter experiences. The new and needed task had already been found in the grandiose program for the industrialization and the rebuilding of the entire structure of the nation, a task which had its roots in Stalin's slogan, "Socialism in a single country." It was about this doctrine that there centered the party struggle which began in the autumn of 1924.

CHAPTER IV

"SOCIALISM IN A SINGLE COUNTRY"

THE PARTY STRUGGLE

THE history of the Russian Social-Democratic Party presents a long record of internal strife and cleavages. One of them, the break between the "Bolshevik" (majority) and the "Menshevik" (minority) wings at the London congress of the party in 1903 was to have vast importance in the future, in spite of the relative insignificance of its immediate causes. At the time it involved questions of tactics rather than of principles, and seemed more like a family quarrel between the party leaders than a real parting of the ways. The acrimonious and bitter division between the Bolsheviks and the Mensheviks continued in the years to come, and there was also little harmony as to the policy to be followed even within the Bolshevik end of the Social-Democratic Party. It will be remembered that in the early days of the revolution of 1917, immediately after the downfall of the monarchy, some who were to be among the most outstanding future leaders of Soviet Russia, including Stalin himself, were entirely out of sympathy with Lenin's program of the dictatorship of the proletariat and the establishment of a Soviet state as the immediate aim of the party, and were willing to lend their support to a democratic republic as a necessary preliminary, and as a protracted stage on the road to socialism. There was also a great deal of disagreement as to the timeliness of the *coup d'état* of October–November, which brought the Bolsheviks into power. Trotsky did not join the Bolshevik Party until 1917 and many of the "old Bolsheviks" found it difficult to reconcile themselves to the prominent part played by this newcomer during the October uprising and the civil war. Even after the Bolsheviks established themselves as the rulers of Holy Russia and assumed the name of the Russian Communist Party, unanimity in their ranks was by no means restored. We have already seen the opposition to the Brest-Litovsk policy of Lenin which developed among the Left Wing communists and in Trotsky, individually. In 1920–1921 the so-called "Labor Opposition" came into being. It is usually associated with the name of Shlyapnikov and it bitterly criticized the New Economic Policy in which it saw a complete surrender of the true revolutionary aims of Bolshevism. The alliance sought by Lenin with the "middle-class" peasants was interpreted by the Labor Opposition as a betrayal of the cause of the proletariat. "We cannot deny," said Madame Kollontai, at the third congress of the Comintern, "that the New Economic Policy makes it possible for capitalism to get on its feet, to be reborn in Russia." And Antanov bluntly declared "The Central Committee of the party has sold the proletariat to the peasants for a mess of pottage." In the opinion of the Left Opposition, the New Economic Policy had completely destroyed the work of the revolution and had condemned "millions of Russian proletarians to the shameful and miserable conditions of a penal institution." Not even world revolution could now save Russia from a growing dominance by the new bourgeois classes—the peasant farmers and the small traders—and a third Russian revolution would be needed if the proletariat was to achieve its aim.[1]

In 1924, with the death of Lenin, the strife within the party entered upon a new and most acute stage, and gradually developed into an open struggle between Trotsky and Stalin. There seemed to be little doubt that the question of personal leadership was not an altogether foreign issue, and that there was no place in the Communist Party for both Stalin and Trotsky. But there was also the most important question of principle involved—the impossibility of reconciling Trotsky's theory of permanent revolution with Stalin's "socialism in one country." At the fourteenth congress of the Communist Party (December, 1925) Trotsky reached a *rapprochement* with the "New Opposition," as it was known, led by Zinoviev and Kamenev, which during the preceding period had opposed the views of both Trotsky and Stalin. In 1926 the New Opposition leaders entered, with Trotsky, into a "bloc" which based itself on its denial that socialism could be established in any

[1] Gaisinsky, *op. cit.*, pp. 70–71.

single country. The struggle between the opposing factions continued at a series of conferences and congresses held by the various Soviet organizations and by the Communist Party. One of the most important among them was the fifteenth conference of the Communist Party which met in October–November, 1926. It practically sealed the doom of the opposition and its verdict was confirmed by the fifteenth congress of the party (December, 1927). In the meantime Trotsky was deprived one by one of his various offices in the Soviet administration. In January, 1925, he was relieved of his duties as Commissar for the Army and Navy, in the autumn of 1926 he was expelled from the Politbureau, and in October, 1927, from the Central Committee of the party. After the fifteenth congress of the party he was exiled to Alma Ata, and in 1929 to Turkey. One of the most picturesque figures of the Russian revolution had thus disappeared—and probably forever— from the Soviet stage. His followers who were slow in doing penance and renouncing the heresy of Trotskyism suffered a similar, if less spectacular, fate.

THE ISSUE

The issue between Stalin and Trotsky was by no means a new one. It enjoyed some popularity with socialist writers in 1905–1906, and again in 1915, in 1921, and during the years following. Then, with the success of the New Economic Policy, the question acquired a new importance and was carried from the field of theory into the field of practical politics.

What was to be the policy of the Soviet Union in the years to come? Its ultimate aim—the abolition of capitalism throughout the world—remained unaltered; but the methods to be followed depended on the answer to the question as to the possibility of establishing socialism in one country alone. If the undertaking was hopeless—and this was the interpretation put upon the views of Trotsky and Zinoviev—then the economic reorganization of the country was obviously a matter of minor importance, and the whole energy of the Soviet Union must be concentrated in a direct and immediate conflict with the capitalist world, the breakdown of which was the only way of reaching the ultimate goal. If, on the other hand, socialism could be established merely in the Soviet Union, in spite of the hostile capitalist environment, then the economic reconstruction of Russia acquired an entirely new significance, both from the merely national point of view, and also from the point of view of the world proletariat. The triumph of a socialist economy, especially while contrasted with the antagonisms of the capitalist world, would be a factor of immeasurable influence in advancing the cause of world communism. What better argument could be devised to favor the purpose the Soviets have at heart than the picture of a prosperous, happy, and self-contained socialist Russia in the midst of capitalist countries suffering from the evils of unemployment, and those crises that are due to the "anarchy of production" and the wastefulness of the capitalist system? It was certainly

worth some purely temporary concessions to the
class enemy. These concessions were not a retreat;
they were merely tactical movements which would
ultimately put the Soviet Union in a much stronger
position. But the difficulty in this very plausible argument was that, in the opinion of a large and by no
means unimportant section of the Communist Party,
it represented a revolutionary and striking departure
from the teaching of Marx, Engels, and Lenin. It
became necessary, therefore, to revise the older doctrine and to convince the party that the originator
of "socialism in a single country" was none other
than Lenin himself. This view received the official
sanction in resolutions passed by party conferences
and congresses, and was made an integral part of
the Soviet articles of faith.

Stalin's new doctrine became the centre of a
stormy controversy which lasted for more than three
years, in spite of the fact that its official acceptance
was proclaimed in a celebrated and much quoted
resolution on, "The aims of the Comintern and the
Russian Communist Party," which was adopted by
the fourteenth conference of the party in April,
1925. It created a vast literature which has run into
thousands of pages. Fortunately for the student who
approaches this truly terrifying monument of controversial writings, the central and fundamental argument is surprisingly simple. This is largely due
to the uniformity of the method used by Soviet
writers on either side, a method which is already
familiar to the reader. To prove anything in the

Soviet Union it is only necessary to prove that this was the view held by Lenin. He is the ultimate and supreme authority. Now Lenin was not directly concerned with the problem of "socialism in a single country" and the passages in his writings which can be interpreted as dealing with it are relatively few. The whole controversy, therefore, resolved itself into a matter of repeating over and over again the same quotations and in refuting them by other and similarly familiar quotations and interpretations. The entire discussion was one of a most disheartening monotony, and represented in itself an extremely eloquent comment on the conditions to which intellectual life had been reduced in the first republic of the proletariat. In presenting the official argument for "socialism in a single country" we shall follow one of its latest and most authoritative versions, Stalin's report on *The Opposition and Domestic Conditions* presented to the fifteenth conference of the Russian Communist Party held from October 26 to November 3, 1926.[2]

THE THREE PROBLEMS

Stalin very properly pointed out that the cleavage which threatened the party centred on the question whether it was possible to build up socialism solely in one country. This question involved three separate problems: (1) Was the victory of socialism in

[2] *Pyatnadtsataya Konferentsya Vsesoyuznoi Kommunisticheskoi Partii Bolshevikov (Fifteenth Conference of the Communist Party of the Soviet Union)*, 26 October–3 November, 1926, verbatim report, Moscow—Leningrad, 1927, pp. 429–456.

Russia possible in spite of the fact that the Soviet Union was still the only country which was living under a régime of proletarian dictatorship, and that the speed of the world revolution had slowed down? (2) If such a victory was possible, could it be called a complete and final victory? (3) If such a victory could not be called final, what were the conditions that were needed to make it final?

It was the first of these three questions which obviously presented the major difficulty and, to give it a satisfactory answer, Stalin saw himself forced to revise some of the accepted views of the founders of "scientific" socialism, Marx and Engels.

ENGELS REVISED

Stalin admitted that in the middle of the last century, in the 'forties, the 'fifties, and the 'sixties, all Marxian socialists, including Marx and Engels, held the opinion that the victory of socialism in one isolated country was utterly out of the question; that this required a simultaneous revolution in at least several of the more advanced and civilized countries. This point of view was perfectly justified at the time; that is, before the appearance of monopolistic capitalism and Lenin's discovery of the law of the "uneven" development of capitalism (about which more will be said below). It was clearly stated in Engels' draft of his *Principles of Communism,* which became the foundation for the *Communist Manifesto.* The draft was written in 1847, but has only recently been published. "Can this [proletarian] revolution take place in merely one country?" asked Engels. "The answer is no. Large-scale industry, by creating the world market, has established so close a connection among all the peoples of the globe, especially in the case of the civilized peoples, that each of them depends on what happens to the other. Then, too, large-scale industry has so levelled the social development in all civilized countries, that everywhere the bourgeosie and the proletariat have become the two determining social classes, and the struggle between them is the chief struggle of our time. The communist revolution, therefore, will not be merely national, but will take place simultaneously in all civilized countries; that is, at least in England, America, France, and Germany. The rapidity of its progress in each of these countries will depend on the degree of development of industry, on the accumulation of wealth, and the amount of means of production in existence. Its progress, therefore, will be particularly slow and difficult in Germany, and particularly rapid and easy in England. It will also exercise a considerable influence upon the other countries of the world and will completely change and much accelerate their former course of developemnt. It is a world revolution and will therefore have the whole world as its arena." [3]

Stalin pointed out that it is highly characteristic that Engels does not even mention Russia. This was

[3] F. Engels, *Principles of Communism*. See Russian edition of *Communist Manifesto*, 1923, p. 317.

perfectly natural, because in the 'forties, when Engels wrote, the Russian proletariat was still non-existent. But a statement which was perfectly justified and sound some eighty years ago was no longer valid under conditions prevailing in the world in the twentieth century. The real greatness of Lenin, as the successor of Marx and Engels, consisted in his refusal to be the slave of the dead letter of Marxism. He had fully grasped the idea frequently emphasized by Marx that his teaching was not a dogma, but a guide for action. Lenin always considered Marxism not as a dogma, but as a method which must be adapted to the new conditions of capitalist development. "The real greatness of Lenin," said Stalin, consists in his raising up openly, honestly, and fearlessly the question of the necessity of a new formula, and in proclaiming the possibility of the victory of the proletarian revolution in separate countries," regardless of the objections this was bound to meet from those who persisted in clinging to the old formula of Marx.

IMPERIALISM

No one, in the opinion of Stalin, could seriously criticize Marx and Engels for failing to foresee a situation which was to arise fifty or sixty years later. There is, however, no longer such excuse for Trotsky and his friends. Lenin was the first among the followers of Marx who took imperialism as the new and last phase of capitalism, and submitted it to a penetrating and truly Marxian analysis. And it led him to the conclusion that the establishment of socialism in a single country was quite feasible. This is what Lenin wrote in 1915: "As an independent slogan, the slogan, 'The United States of the World,' would be, however, hardly a suitable one; first, because it merges with socialism; secondly, because it might create a mistaken impression as to the possibility of the victory of socialism in one country alone, and the relations of such a country to other countries. The unevenness of its economic and political development is an absolute law of capitalism. From this it follows that the victory of socialism is originally possible in a few or even in one separate capitalistic country. The victorious proletariat of this country, having expropriated the capitalists and organized socialist production at home, would rise against the remaining capitalist world, attracting to itself the exploited classes in other countries, organizing their revolts against the capitalists, and if necessary using even military force against the exploiting classes and their states." Because "the free association of nations in socialism is impossible without a more or less protracted and stubborn struggle of the socialist republics against the other states." [4]

What is this law of uneven development of capitalism from which, in the opinion of Stalin, Lenin deduced the possibility of establishing capitalism in one country? As stated by Stalin, it may be summarized as follows: Lenin takes for his point of departure a number of facts which are established by

[4] N. Lenin, Vol. XVIII, p. 133.

his analysis of the existing conditions. He finds that the old pre-monopolistic capitalism has been transferred into imperialism; that the development of the world economy proceeds under conditions of a wild struggle, between the chief imperialistic groups, for territories, markets, raw materials, and so on; that the partition of the world into spheres of influence controlled by the imperialistic groups has been completed; that the development of the capitalist countries proceeds unevenly, that is, they do not follow one another or pursue a parallel course; but that its course is highly irregular and manifests itself in crowding out the countries which are too far ahead and in pushing new countries into the front rank; that under these conditions the development of the capitalist countries unavoidably leads to conflicts, and to wars among the capitalist nations for a new redistribution of the world they have already divided; that these conflicts and wars lead to the weakening of imperialism; that, as a consequence, the world front of imperialism can be easily broken in certain of the countries; and that therefore the victory of socialism in one country only is made possible.

To illustrate the validity of this argument, examples are drawn from the recent history of the world. England, until lately, was the leading imperialist country. Then Germany came in and demanded a place in the sun at the expense of other nations and especially of England. The immediate effect of this conflict of interests was the war of 1914–1918. Since the great war, America has been vastly in the lead, leaving England and the other European nations far behind. It was beyond doubt that this situation would lead to new conflicts and wars.

The experience of the Russian revolution indicated that under modern conditions the front of the imperialists would not necessarily break in the countries which had the most highly developed industry, as suggested by Engels, but in those where the proletariat had powerful allies in other social groups; for instance, among the peasants, as was the case in Russia. The chain of imperialism would break at the weakest link. It was quite possible that the next victory of the revolution would take place in a country like India, where the proletariat had a potential ally against the imperialist oppressor in the movement for national emancipation.

LENIN VS. TROTSKY

These opinions of Lenin, Stalin pointed out, were immediately contested by Trotsky. "The only more or less concrete historical argument against the slogan, 'The United States of Europe,'" Trotsky wrote in 1915, "appeared in Switzerland in the *Sotsial Demokrat* [then the official organ of the Bolsheviks, and a journal published in Russian]. The argument lay in the following sentence: 'The unevenness of its political and economic development is an absolute law of capitalism.' From it the *Sotsial Demokrat* drew the conclusion that the victory of socialism was possible in one country only, and that it was therefore superfluous to make the dictatorship of the proletariat in each separate country dependent on the creation of 'the United States of Europe.'] That the capitalist development of the various countries proceeds unevenly is beyond doubt. But this very unevenness is itself uneven. The capitalist levels of England, Austria, Germany, and France are not the same. But when compared with Africa and Asia, all these countries represent a capitalist Europe which is ripe for social revolution. That no country should wait for others in its struggle is an elementary principle which it is useful and necessary to repeat, lest the idea of parallel international action should be replaced by the idea of delaying international action.] When we do not wait for others, we begin and we continue the struggle on our own national soil, fully confident that our initiative will stimulate the struggle in other countries; and if this could not be hoped for, then it would be hopeless to expect—as is proved by both historical experiences and by theoretical considerations—that, for instance, a revolution in Russia could maintain itself when confronted with capitalist Europe, or a socialist Germany could remain isolated in the midst of a capitalist world." [5]

Stalin pointed out that Trotsky's views flagrantly contradicted those of Lenin. While Lenin said that the proletariat which would seize power in one country would not only be able to maintain itself but

[5] L. Trotsky, *Sochinenya (Works)*, Vol. III, Part I, pp. 89–90; this article appeared first in the newspaper *Nashe Slovo* and was reprinted in a collection of his essays under the title *Programma Mira (Program of Peace)* in August, 1917.

would go farther—it would expropriate the wealth of the capitalists and organize a socialist economy in order to be able to lend its support to the proletariat in other capitalist countries—Trotsky, on the contrary, believed that unless the triumph of the socialist revolution in one country was not immediately followed by a successful revolution in other countries, then the victorious proletariat was doomed to lose control of the government, to say nothing of finding it impossible to establish socialism. Lenin pictured the victorious proletariat as an active force, full of initiative, organizing socialism and ready to help other countries. Trotsky saw it as a purely passive mass, depending on the help of an immediate revolution in other countries, and "camping" in government offices under the threat of an immediate loss of power.

These fundamental divergencies of opinion between Lenin and Trotsky, Stalin maintained, did not disappear in the course of the years that followed. In 1921, in connection with the New Economic Policy and the charges made by the Labor Opposition that the Soviet Government had betrayed the cause of socialism, Lenin stated on several occasions that the New Economic Policy was not an abandonment of the old aims, but merely a change in methods, to lay "the socialist foundation of our economy". . ."together with the peasants" . . ."under the leadership of the working class."

As if deliberately trying to refute Lenin's views, in January, 1922, Trotsky published a new edition of his *1905,* provided with an introduction in which he said that the proletariat that had seized power "would enter into hostile conflict not only with all the bourgeois groups which supported it during the early stages of its revolutionary struggle, but also with the great masses of the peasantry whose collaboration had brought it to power, and that the contradictions involved in a workers' government in a backward country with a predominantly peasant population could find their solution only on the internationl scale and in the arena of the world proletarian revolution."

About a year later, in 1922, Lenin returned to the question of socialism in Russian in a speech delivered before the Moscow Soviet. "Socialism," he said, "is now no longer a question of the remote future, or an abstract picture, or an icon. We still hold our old and very unfavorable view of the icon. We have dragged socialism into everyday life, and now we must see what we are to do about it. This is the problem of the day, the problem of our era. Will you allow me to close by expressing the belief that in spite of the difficulties of this problem, in spite of its differing from our former problems, and in spite of all the work it will demand of us, we shall all together—not to-morrow but in the course of a few years—we shall all together and at any cost find a solution to this problem so that from the Russia of the N. E. P. will emerge a socialist Russia."[6]

To this statement of Lenin's, Stalin again finds an

[6] N. Lenin, Vol. XVIII, Part 2, p. 108.

answer in Trotsky's introduction to his *Programma Mira (Program of Peace)*, published in 1922. "The contention which appears several times in the *Program of Peace*," wrote Trotsky, "that the proletarian revolution cannot maintain itself victoriously within national limits, will, perhaps, seem to some readers as having been refuted by the five-year experience of our Soviet republic. But such a conclusion would be unjustified. The fact that a workers' government has maintained itself in a single country, and that in a backward country, bears witness to the immense power of the proletariat which, in other more advanced and more civilized countries, will be able to perform real miracles. But having maintained ourselves in the political and military sense, as a state, we have not yet reached or even approached the creation of a socialist society. . . . As long as other European countries are controlled by the bourgeoisie, we are forced in our struggle against economic isolation to seek an understanding with the capitalist world; at the same time it may be said with confidence that such understandings, at the best, will help us to heal this or that economic wound, to take this or that step forward, but that the real progress of socialist economic measures in Russia will become possible only after the victory of the proletariat in the principal European countries.'

The most striking expression of Lenin's views on the possibilities of "socialism in a single country" was given by him, in the opinion of Stalin, in two articles written shortly before his death, and they must be regarded as his political testament. In an article written early in 1923, Lenin criticized the rigid attitude of Sukhanov and other "heroes of the Second International," who failed to grasp the full meaning of Marx's revolutionary dialectics, and held wholly to the outward Marxian formulæ. "How infinitely conventional," wrote Lenin, "is their contention, which they have learned by heart during the course of the western European revolutions and which declares that we are not yet ripe for socialism, that we have not mastered, to use the expression of some of the 'erudite' gentlemen among them, the objective economic requisites for the building up of socialism." Lenin advanced the view that there is no general scheme of revolution applicable to every case, but that much depends on local conditions. "If the establishment of socialism demands a definite cultural level although no one can say what this level is," he wrote, "then why should we not master by revolutionary methods the requisites needed for reaching this level? After that, too, on the platform of the government by the workers and peasants embodied in the Soviet system, why should we not proceed to make good the gap which separates us from the other nations?"[7]

Even more importance was attached by Stalin to a paragraph which appears in the last article, *On Cooperative Societies,* written by Lenin before his death. "Indeed," said Lenin in this article, "state control of all the large means of production, a gov-

[7] N. Lenin, Vol. XVIII, Part 2, pp. 118–119.

ernment fully controlled by millions of the proletariat, the alliance between the proletariat and the many millions of small and very small peasant farmers, a situation in which the proletariat is assured of its leadership of the peasantry, and so on—is this not all that is necessary in order that building from the coöperative societies and the coöperative societies alone—which we used to look down upon as low commercial organizations and which even now, under the N. E. P., we are still entitled to look down upon in the same way—is this not all that is necessary in order to set up a complete socialist society? This is not yet the socialist society, completely constructed, but it is all that is necessary, and is sufficient for it. . . . If it were not for our international relations and if it were not our duty to fight for our position on a world scale, I would be willing to say that the centre of our activities is being shifted to cultural work."[8]

This was interpreted as an irrefutable proof that in the opinion of Lenin the establishment of "socialism in a single country" was quite feasible.

THE FINAL VICTORY OF SOCIALISM

But does it mean the final victory of socialism? To this question Stalin gives a negative answer. The Soviet Union has succeeded in destroying Russian capitalism and is perfectly capable of organizing a socialist community; but this is still no guarantee against the danger of intervention and the possibility of restoration. The Union is living in a hostile

[8] N. Lenin, Vol. XVIII, Part 2, pp. 140–144.

capitalist environment. Its very existence exercises a tremendous revolutionizing influence in the world. To imagine that the capitalist governments will become reconciled to the growth and the increasing power of the Soviet state is to leave the realm of realities for the realm of illusions. Capitalist hatred of the Russian revolution is daily increasing. In order therefore to rid the Union of the danger of intervention and restoration, one must replace the present capitalist environment with a socialist environment; and that can be obtained only through the victory of the proletariat in at least several capitalist countries. This is why the victory of socialism in Russia is not considered as an aim in itself, but as a method, as a stepping-stone to the triumph of the proletarian revolution in other countries. This view, again, is supported by quotations from Lenin. "We live not only in a state, but in a system of states, and the existence of the Soviet republic side by side with imperialist states for any great length of time is unthinkable. In the end either one or the other must win. In the meantime, a series of the most terrible collisions between the Soviet republic and the bourgeois states is inevitable. This means that the proletariat, as the dominating class, if it seeks and actually intends to exercise dominion, must prove it by its military organization." [9] From this Stalin draws the conclusion that the danger of intervention exists, and will continue to exist, for many years to come. It is another question whether the capitalist coun-

[9] N. Lenin, Vol. XVI, p. 102.

tries will actually dare to undertake seriously to intervene in Russia. Much hangs on the attitude of
the working classes in the bourgeois nations. The
international position of the Soviet Union largely depends on the sympathy of the international proletariat. If it were not for it, many attempts to organize expeditions against the Bolshevik state would
have already been made. Lenin was quite right,
therefore, when he said that "So long as our Soviet
republic remains a lonely borderland of the capitalist
world, just for so long would it be ridiculous and
Utopian to imagine . . . that this or that danger
will disappear. For so long as such fundamental antagonisms remain, naturally the dangers will also
remain. One cannot run away from them." [10] And
this is why Lenin has declared that "final victory can
take place only on a world scale, and only by the
joint efforts of the workers of all countries." [11]

What, then, is meant by the victory of "socialism
in a single country"? It means the establishment of
the dictatorship of the proletariat and the creation
of a socialist economy which triumphs over the capitalist elements within the country. And what is
meant by the final victory of socialism? It means a
complete guarantee against intervention and restoration, and one that can be obtained only through
socialist revolution in at least certain other countries. The victory of socialism in one country alone
means the ending of internal antagonisms, which is

[10] N. Lenin, Vol. XVII, pp. 408–409.
[11] N. Lenin, Vol. XV, p. 287.

quite feasible in a country like Russia; the final victory of socialism means the solution of international
antagonisms between the socialist country and the
capitalist countries, and that can be achieved only
through an international proletarian revolution.

THE IMPORTANCE OF THE NEW DOCTRINE

The feeling may arise—and it has probably arisen
in the mind of the reader—that all discussion as to
the possibility of establishing socialism in a single
country is entirely preposterous, and that the Communist Party would have done better to concentrate
on practical work instead of wasting its time in sterile
and futile controversy. This criticism was anticipated
by Stalin, who declared that it betrays an attitude
which has nothing in common with Leninism.

The Soviet Union cannot move forward, he declared, unless it knows where, and has a definite purpose before it. It is impossible to establish socialism without possessing confidence that the task is a
feasible one. The Communist Party can only direct
the socialist reconstruction of Russia if it clearly
sees the road ahead. It cannot accept the view of
Bernstein that it is the motion forward, the action,
and not the purpose, that really matters. On the
contrary, the Communist Party must frame its action in such a manner that it meets the fundamental
aims of the class struggle. This alone can keep it out
of the morass of opportunism. Without a clear idea
of the possibilities of socialist construction, without
assurance that it can be achieved, the masses of the

proletariat cannot whole-heartedly participate in it, they cannot lead the peasantry. The inevitable result of the weakening of confidence in the outlook for socialism would be the strengthening of the capitalist elements in the country. It would also lead to a slowing down of the revolutionary movement in other countries. It must be kept in mind that the world proletariat follows the progress of socialist reconstruction in Russia with intense interest and that it hopes proportionately for its success. The labor delegations that in numbers flock to Russia from every corner of the world, and the enthusiasm with which they study every new development, is in itself a proof of the tremendous importance of Russia's struggle "on the economic front" from the point of view of the advancement of the world revolution. Anyone who urges to go more slowly in establishing socialism in the Union is at the same time undermining the confidence which the international proletariat has in it. That is, he is breaking one of the fundamental canons of the proletarian international. Lenin was quite right when he wrote the following lines: "In the present we are exercising our chief pressure upon the international revolution through our economic policy. Upon the Soviet republic are the eyes of all the workers in all the countries of the world, without exception and without exaggeration. . . . In this respect the struggle is already being carried on on the world scale. When we settle this problem —then we shall win on the world scale, unquestionably and finally. This is why questions of economic reconstruction for us take on exceptional importance. On this front we must gain the victory by a slow, a gradual—(it cannot be fast!)—a slow but stubborn progress and advance." [12]

Stalin maintains, therefore, that the discussion of the possibility of establishing socialism in a single country is by no means futile, academic discussion. We are dealing with a most pressing and actual problem; and upon its solution depends the success of the work that has been undertaken by the Soviet government, what it is really to accomplish, and the methods by which it is to be carried on in the near future. [13]

[12] N. Lenin, Vol. XVIII, Part 1, p. 282.

[13] It would seem that the real precursor of Stalin in framing the doctrine of socialism in a single country was Vollmar, who, in 1878, published an article entitled, "The Isolated Socialist State." "Under the conditions now prevailing," he wrote, referring to the lack of uniformity in the development of the capitalist nations, "conditions which will also be found in the future, so far as we can foresee, the hypothesis of simultaneous victories for socialism in all civilized countries is absolutely excluded. . . . We are driven back upon the isolated socialist state; and as to it, I hope I have proved that if it is not the only such possibility, it is at least the one most likely to be set up." This part of Vollmar's assertion was in line with the view then prevailing among the Marxian socialists that dictatorships of the proletariat in the various countries need not arise simultaneously. But he went a great deal farther, thus establishing a partial kinship between his doctrine and that since advanced by Stalin. Socialist Germany, in the opinion of Vollmar, will maintain close economic relations with the capitalist nations and will in this way take advantage of her lower cost of production and her superior technique. His whole theory was based on his assumption that socialism and capitalism could exist peacefully together. The progress of the socialist state would demonstrate its immense advantages in the matter of organization for production, and the necessity for world revolution would disappear of itself. Socialism would triumph over capitalism through the market, through the instrumentality of lower prices resulting from lower costs. (Léon Trotsky, *L'internationale communiste après Lénine*, Paris, 1930,

TROTSKY'S CRITICISM

We know already that Stalin's "socialism in a single country" found itself in irreconcilable conflict with Trotsky's "permanent revolution," with which the reader is familiar. The central idea of the matter, it will be remembered, consists in the close interdependence of the nations of the world, which makes it impossible for one country to develop and maintain, for any length of time, an economic and social system as fundamentally different from that of other nations as socialism is from capitalism. Nor were Trotsky and his friends willing to concede that Lenin was the real author of the new doctrine which, in the opinion of Stalin, was his chief claim to greatness. They, too, had studied the writings of the Master and found in them plenty of ammunition to support their views, which were the very opposite of those of Stalin. Trotsky, for instance, unearthed the following interesting statement made by Lenin in the draft of an article he was planning to write in 1905: "The labor movement wins in the democratic revolution. The bourgeoisie goes over to the counter-revolution. Among the peasantry the whole of its well-to-do class as well as many in its 'middle' class decide to be prudent, they settle down again and side with the counter-revolution, so that they will be able to wrest power from the hands of the proletariat and the poorer peasants. . . . The strug-

pp. 136–137.) The negation of the necessity of world revolution is, of course, in contradiction to the views held by Stalin.

gle would have been almost hopeless for the Russian proletariat alone, and its defeat would have been inevitable . . . if the European socialist revolution had not come to the rescue of the Russian proletariat." [14] Trotsky remarks, and it would seem not without good reason, that this statement sounds very much like an expression of Trotskyism in its most "impudent" mood.

And again: "The Russian [democratic] revolution," Lenin writes, "cannot by its own means retain and consolidate its acquisitions . . . unless a socialist revolution takes place in the West. Without this condition, a restoration is inescapable irrespective of whether municipalization, nationalization, or mere partition [of land among the peasants] is carried through, because the small owner, under any form of tenure and ownership, will be the mainstay of the restoration. After the complete victory of the democratic revolution, the small owner is bound to turn against the proletariat." [15]

The same views were held by Lenin, Trotsky maintained, after the establishment of the Soviet rule in Russia. "The complete victory of the socialist revolution is impossible in merely one country," said Lenin on November 8, 1918; "it will require the active collaboration of at least several advanced countries, among which Russia cannot be included."

[14] *Leninsky Sbornik (Lenin's Symposium)* published by the Lenin Institute, Vol. V, Leningrad, 1926, quoted in verbatim report of the fifteenth conference of the Communist Party of the Soviet Union, pp. 516–517.
[15] N. Lenin, Vol. IX, p. 415.

And Trotsky insisted that Lenin's statement did not apply to the "final victory," in the sense of a guarantee from foreign intervention, but to the actual collaboration of at least several advanced countries. What Lenin had in mind was that the internal contradictions resulting from the backwardness of Russia could not be ended without world revolution. That is, Trotsky felt, there was complete agreement between Lenin and himself.[16]

Other evidence was produced to support this point of view. "I am aware that there are learned men," wrote Lenin, on May 14, 1918, "men believing themselves very clever, and even calling themselves socialists, who maintain that we should not have assumed governmental responsibilities until revolution had been triumphant in all countries. They do not realize that by talking as they do they renounce revolution and side with the bourgeoisie. To wait until the laboring classes will bring about revolution on a world scale means that we must be all condemned to a state in which all we can do is sit motionless and wait. That is nonsense. The difficulties of revolution are well known. Having started with a brilliant success in one country, revolution may have to go through periods of great trials, because the final victory is only possible on the world scale and only through the combined efforts of the workers in all countries." [17]

"In countries of developed capitalism," said Lenin,

[16] Verbatim report of the fifteenth conference of the Communist Party of the Soviet Union, pp. 523–524.
[17] N. Lenin, Vol. XV, p. 287.

at the tenth congress of the Russian Communist Party in 1921, "there is a class of hired agricultural laborers that has grown up in the course of decades. Only in such countries where this class is sufficiently developed, is transition from capitalism to socialism possible. We have stressed the fact in many of our writings, and in all our pronouncements, that this is not the case in Russia, that in Russia industrial labor is in a minority, and the small farmer is an immense majority. Socialist revolution in such a country can be finally successful only under the following two conditions: First, support by some timely social revolution in one or several advanced countries; and, second, an understanding between . . . the proletariat and the majority of the peasant population. . . . We know that only an understanding with the peasantry can preserve the socialist revolution in Russia until the revolution in other countries takes place." [18] Trotsky pointed out that Lenin here spoke of two conditions requisite for the final victory of the socialist revolution in any single country, the first being a *timely* socialist revolution in one or several advanced countries; and that this was held particularly important for a backward country, like Russia. [19]

[18] N. Lenin, Vol. XVIII, Part I, pp. 137–138.

[19] Trotsky had also pointed out that it was Lenin who, in 1921, approved of the constitution of the organization of Communist Youth, as prepared by a committee over which Bukharin presided. Article 4 of the constitution reads as follows: "The control of the government of the U.S.S.R. is already in the hands of the working class. In the course of the three years of its heroic struggle against capitalism the proletariat has maintained and strengthened the power of the Soviets. Although Rus-

Trotsky admitted, of course, that the Soviet Union was making remarkable progress along the road of economic recovery, but he pleaded that the actual significance of this should not be exaggerated. According to the estimates of the Supreme Economic Council, the country would reach the economic level of 1913 only in 1930. But what was the level of 1913? It was the level of misery, backwardness, barbarism. It had nothing to do with real socialism, which meant the elimination of antagonisms between the cities and the agricultural countryside, general well-being, material comfort, culture. All this was still a thing of the very remote future. Lenin expressed similar views as late as 1922. After giving the highest praise to the achievement of Bolshevism in establishing the first Soviet state, one which had opened a new era in the history of the human race, he proceeded with characteristic frankness: "But we have not yet completed even the foundation of a socialist economy. It is still possible for what we have done to be taken away from us again by the hostile forces of expiring capitalism. We must clearly realize and openly admit this, for nothing is more dangerous than illusions (and light-headedness, especially at high altitudes). There is, moreover, nothing terrible, and nothing offering legitimate reason for even the slightest depression in the recognition

sia has immense natural resources, she is nevertheless an industrially backward country with a predominately petty bourgeois population. She can attain to socialism only through the proletarian world revolution: we have now entered the period of the latter." (Léon Trotsky, *L'internationale communiste après Lénine,* pp. 131–132.)

of this bitter truth, because we have always professed and proclaimed, as the elementary truth of Marxism, that the victory of socialism will require the concerted efforts of the workers of several advanced countries." [20]

The article, *On Coöperative Societies,* quoted by Stalin [21] as the irrefutable evidence of Lenin's sanction of "socialism in a single country," Trotsky continues, really meant something quite different. What Lenin actually did in this article was to enumerate some of the conditions which were essential to the establishment of socialism. He listed five of them: the ownership of the means of production—one; government by the proletariat—two; an alliance between the proletariat and the peasantry—three; proletarian leadership of the peasantry—four; and coöperative societies—five. This last, however, was not a comprehensive one. No communist would maintain that socialism could be established in *any* separate country. If, for instance, these five condition could be found in Bulgaria, no one would really admit that Bulgaria was in a position to set up a complete socialist system. There were other conditions that were, obviously, essential to the success of socialism in any particular country, such as geographical position, natural resources, technical knowledge, and culture. Lenin spoke merely of the conditions relating to the form of government, of ownership, of organization. He never meant his list

[20] N. Lenin, Vol. XX, Part 2, p. 487.
[21] See *above,* pp. 142–143.

to be complete and exhaustive. His article, *On Co-operative Societies,* merely amplified his earlier views; it certainly did not revise them.[22]

One of the puzzling features of the controversy over "socialism in a single country" is Stalin's own recent and rather unexpected conversion to this doctrine. This is what he wrote in April, 1924: "The overthrow of the political power of the bourgeoisie and the transfer of such power to the proletariat in one country does not yet guarantee the complete victory of socialism. The chief purpose of socialism —the organization of socialist production—still remains to be achieved. Is it possible to solve this problem, to achieve the final victory of socialism in any single country without the joint effort of several advanced countries? No, this is impossible. The overthrow of the political power of the bourgeoisie can be accomplished by the efforts of one country, as we know this from the experience of our revolution. But for the final victory of socialism, for the organization of socialist production, the efforts of one country, especially of a peasant country like Russia, are not enough; this requires the efforts of the proletarians of several advanced countries. The development and support of the revolutions in other countries is one of the essential tasks of the victorious revolution. The victorious revolution, therefore, must consider itself not as a self-contained unit, but as a subsidiary to, as a method for, the

---

[22] Verbatim report of the fifteenth conference of the Communist Party of the Soviet Union, pp. 527–528.

advancement of the victory of the proletariat in other countries." [23]

This certainly was a clear-cut statement which did not seem to be compatible with the view expressed by Stalin a few months later. Nevertheless he explained it away in another article written in December of the same year, which contained the fundamental ideas of the doctrine of "socialism in a single country" with which we are now familiar. It introduced the now celebrated distinction between the victory of socialism in only one country, which is declared quite feasible, and the final victory, which means the removal of the danger of foreign intervention.[24] One can hardly blame Trotsky and his friends very severely for finding it difficult to accept this explanation. They could not possibly overlook the fact that in his earlier article Stalin did not even mention intervention, but stated very clearly that the organization of socialist production, the real purpose of socialism, could not be achieved in a peasant country like Russia. This, Trotsky said, was a very sound point of view. It is ridiculous to represent the situation in such a manner as would make it seem that the Russian communists were building a house and their enemies were breaking

[23] J. Stalin, *O. Lenine i Leninisme* (*About Lenin and Leninism*), Moscow, 1924, p. 60.

[24] J. Stalin, *Oktayabrskaya revolyutsya i taktika russkikh kommunistov* (*The October Revolution and the Tactics of the Russian Communists*), Moscow, 1924, reprinted in J. Stalin, *Ob oppozitsii* (*On the Opposition*), Moscow—Leningrad, 1928, pp. 155-159. *Cf.* also J. Stalin, *Voprosi i otveti* (*Questions and Answers*), Moscow, 1925.

their windows from the outside. Intervention is war, and war is another expression of the political struggle which itself is determined by economic factors. The problem, therefore, embraces the entire field of economic relations between the Soviet Union and the capitalist world. It is childish to imagine that the relations between Russia and other countries are limited to intervention. They are infinitely deeper and more comprehensive.

The whole problem of establishing socialism in one country alone, according to Trotsky, belongs to the field of metaphysics, not of practical politics. If we admit for a moment that socialism in a single country is possible, the question arises, what is Europe going to do in the meantime? The completion of the socialist structure in the U. S. S. R., in the opinion of Trotsky, will take at least from thirty to fifty years. If, during this period, the European proletariat wins a definite victory, the problem will naturally solve itself and the future of communism will be safe. But if this does not take place, what will take place? Trotsky suggests three alternatives: (1) The present equilibrium between the proletariat and the bourgeoisie will be maintained; it is, however, so unstable that its continuation for another thirty, forty, or fifty years is out of the question. Trotsky therefore rejects this possibility. (2) Capitalism will recover and continue to develop, thus proving that it has not yet completely fulfilled its historical mission. This assumption is against the fundamentals of communism, and if proved to be correct it would mean that Bolshevism had come too early. In this case communism would be destroyed by capitalism, which has at its disposal a strong military machine and controls labor through the corrupted labor aristocracy. (3) Capitalism is declining; then why should labor not succeed in winning a complete victory and in establishing the dictatorship of the proletariat? What pessimism! There is no political or theoretical reason which would lead one to believe that it is easier to establish socialism in one isolated country with the help of the peasantry, than it is for the proletariat of the advanced European nations to seize power. If this argument is well founded, Trotsky declares, the problem of socialism in a single country does not arise at all.[25]

ZINOVIEV'S ATTITUDE

It would be superfluous for our purposes to attempt a detailed survey of all the points of criticism raised against the doctrine of socialism in one country alone. What has been already said will suffice to give an idea of the conflicting points of view and of the cumbersome and questionable method of quoting and interpreting Lenin which was used on both sides. Broadly speaking, during the earlier part of the controversy the chief emphasis of Stalin's critics was upon the domestic difficulties encountered by socialism in Russia, difficulties which arose from

[25] Verbatim report of the fifteenth conference of the Communist Party of the Soviet Union, pp. 531–533.

the low basis of education and cultural levels in the country. In the latter part of the discussion, especially at the seventh enlarged plenum of the Executive Committee of the Comintern in December, 1926,[26] the international obstacles inherent in the close interdependence of the nations of the world received special attention, and were used as the main argument against the new doctrine. The argument itself is already familiar to us and it formed, it will be remembered, an integral part of Trotsky's theory of permanent revolution.

A few words may be added on the attitude of Zinoviev, partly because of the leading rôle he still played in the Comintern and partly because of the remarkable shift which took place in his views. In 1924 Zinoviev was one of the vehement opponents of Trotskyism and he was the author of the resolution adopted by the fourteenth conference of the Communist Party in April, 1925, which was the first authoritative expression of the doctrine of socialism in a single country. He supported it in an eloquent address which could but meet with the unreserved approval of Stalin.[27] In ensuing months, however, his views suffered a striking change and, as we know, in 1926 he entered with Trotsky into a

[26] *Puti morovoi revolyutsii (The Ways of the World Revolution)*, verbatim report of the seventh enlarged plenum of the Executive Committee of the Communist International, Moscow, 1927, Vols. I and II.

[27] G. Zinoviev, *Chastichnaya stabilizatsya kapitalisma i zadachi Kominterna (Partial Stabilization of Capitalism and the Aims of the Comintern)*, in *Kommunisticheski Internatsional*, May, 1925, No. 5, pp. 28–46.

"bloc" which uncompromisingly opposed the very doctrine he did so much to promote. In the summer of 1926 he went so far as to declare that "the teaching of Marx, Engels, and Lenin on the international proletarian revolution has nothing in common with Stalin's opportunist nonsense about socialism in one sole country." [28] The reason for this change, it may be surmised, was Zinoviev's belated realization of the fact that the acceptance of Stalin's views would unavoidably lead to the weakening of the interest of the Soviet Union in the promotion of world revolution which he had particularly at heart, and the concentration of all its efforts on the problems of domestic reconstruction.

The fifteenth conference of the Communist Party in October–November, 1926, found Zinoviev fighting Stalin on the side of Trotsky. He was particularly shocked by Stalin's attempt to revise the teaching of Marx and Engels. He refused to subscribe to the opinion that the principles on which the *Communist Manifesto* was based are now antiquated and out of date. No such statement, he maintained, could be discovered in the writings of Lenin. On the contrary, this was what Lenin wrote in 1918: "The great founders of socialism, Marx and Engels, having observed, during the course of decades, the development of the labor movement and the growth of the world socialist revolution, saw clearly that the change from capitalism will demand a long

[28] G. Zinoviev, *Dvadtsat odno uslovie Leninskago Kominterna* (*Twenty-one Conditions of Lenin's Comintern*), quoted in Gaisinsky, *op. cit.*, p. 140.

transitional period, during which there will be a pitiless 'scrapping' and destruction both of all that is old and of all the institutions of capitalism; and that this will require the collaboration of the workers of all countries, who will be compelled to unite their efforts to achieve the final victory. And they said: 'The French will begin, the Germans will complete the work.' . . . We see to-day a different combination of the forces of international socialism. We say that it is easier to begin the movement in those countries which do not belong to that ring of exploiting countries which have the best opportunities for plundering, and for buying off those who have reached the top in the laboring classes . . . ; we can clearly see now how the development of the revolution will proceed; the Russian has begun, the German, French, English will complete the work, and socialism will triumph." [29] "This was, indeed, a revision of the program of Marx and Engels," said Zinoviev, "but it had nothing to do with socialism in a single country, and it did not affect the fundamentals of the world revolution. As to Marx and Engels themselves, they never abandoned their original view that the only way to communism was through an international revolution. Even as early as December 31, 1848, after the publication of the *Communist Manifesto,* Marx wrote a sentence that we have already quoted in part: "An economic *coup d'état* in any country of the European continent or even in the whole of the European continent without

[29] N. Lenin, Vol. XV, pp. 87–88.

England is merely a tempest in a teacup." And as late as 1885 Engels emphasized the fact that the principal theoretical link between the members of the first communist organization was their belief that only a European revolution could be victorious.[30]

Russia, of course, would establish socialism, Zinoviev declared, but she would establish it in collaboration with the other nations of the world, in collaboration with the world revolution; this revolution was bound to come. And Lenin had indicated clearly what was to be done in the meantime. "Our purpose, so long as we are isolated," he said, in April, 1918, "consists in preserving the revolution, in safeguarding for it at least one stronghold of socialism, however weak and insignificant it may be, until revolution takes place in other countries, until its other detachments arrive."[31] This is the true and only significance of the Soviet Union and it has nothing in common with the preposterous idea of establishing socialism in one country alone.

THE NEW NATIONALISM

The discussion which took place in 1925–1926 provided ample evidence that Zinoviev's feeling that the new doctrine would result in the relegating to the background world revolution and the growth of a new nationalism was not without foundation. The numerous manifestations of this nationalistic spirit,

[30] Verbatim report of the fifteenth conference of the Communist Party of the Soviet Union, pp. 571–573.
[31] N. Lenin, Vol. XV, p. 232.

some of which we shall have to note, have resulted
in Stalin's being accused of creating a frame of mind
in the Russian Communist Party that was essentially
and fundamentally un-Marxian. It is often said
that the Russian communists are encouraged to look
upon themselves as the leaders of a chosen people
and are imbued with a messianic spirit sufficient
to establish their intellectual kinship with some
of those Russian reactionaries, such as the Slavo-
phils, who, to the socialists, are most abhorrent.
But what is even worse, absorption in domestic
problems is supposed to have developed in the
Russian Communist Party a tendency, purely bourgeois, toward "national self-sufficiency," as opposed
to their former ideal, that of being the torch-
bearers, but merely the torch-bearers, of that great
socialist revolution which will be on a world scale.
The new conception of the part of the Soviet Union
is to play in bringing about world revolution cannot but be revolting to those who were the leaders
in the "romantic" period of the revolution. In the
autumn of 1926, at the fifteenth conference of the
Communist Party, this was clearly stated by Stalin
and some of his lieutenants.

We are already familiar with Stalin's views on the
subject. Bukharin, who was among Stalin's most
enthusiastic supporters during this period, stressed
the opinion that although the pressure brought upon
Russia by the capitalist countries was a grave ob-
stacle, it was by no means an insurmountable one.
The Russian revolution was to him primarily an

integral part of the world revolution, but his attitude was in a sense different from that of Zinoviev.
As he saw it, it was by strengthening the position
of the Soviet Union that the world revolution could
best be promoted. No country had given more
moral support to the revolution in China, the trade
unions of no country had given more help to the
British miners in their strike; it was impossible to
deny that "the Russian Communist Party is, was,
and will remain the chief stronghold of world revolution." [32]

Ossinsky declared that the Soviet Union was establishing socialism not only for itself but for the
world proletariat "because the experience gained in
establishing a socialist economy, experience that is
continuously enlarged in Russia, will be used by
the world proletariat. In this sense, and merely
in our own country, we are already establishing world
socialism." This also applied not merely to economics, but to other fields; for instance, to the administration of affairs of state, something that would
likewise prove to be a mine of practical instruction
for every new Soviet republic. This was similarly
true of the military organization of the Soviet Union,
of the Red army, and especially of the cultural
work which was being done in Russia. It belonged to
the proletariat of the world. "Even to-day," Ossinsky said, "without undue self-glorification we are
bound to recognize that here, in the U. S. S. R., we

[32] Verbatim report of the fifteenth conference of the Communist Party of the Soviet Union, p. 603.

have created a world centre of socialist culture." [33]

Molotov, Lenin's successor in the office of President of the Council of People's Commissars, reiterated the already familiar argument as to the necessity of a definite assurance that the task undertaken by the Russian proletariat could be successfully fulfilled [the elimination of these endless repetitions is, perhaps, one of the most difficult tasks which the student of the Stalin-Trotsky controversy has to face]. There must be no doubt that the Soviet Union could, and would, achieve the goal it had set itself. At the same time, he said, one must also remember that communism was rapidly spreading among the working classes in all capitalist countries, that the success of Russia's great enterprise was a powerful factor in stimulating the proletarian revolution, and that every new achievement of the Soviet Union would make the assistance it was giving the world proletariat more direct and more effective. It was quite possible, therefore, that the triumph of socialism in the U. S. S. R. would coincide or, at any rate, would be necessarily followed by the victory of world-wide socialism. "This means that in case of delays in the socialist revolution in other countries, the victory of socialism in one country [the U. S. S. R.] will, in the historical ending of modern imperialism, merge in the final victory; that is, in such a victory as will remove not only the internal, but also the international, obstacles to complete socialist de-

[33] *Ibid.*, p. 616.

velopment and will thus lead to the victory of communism. . . . The policy of our party is, and will remain, the policy of the victory of socialism in our country, and, at the same time, the policy of the final victory of socialism in the world at large." [34]

These pronouncements of the Soviet leaders were little more than the restatement of the views set forth by Stalin in the fourteenth congress of the Communist Party in December, 1925. In his report to the congress on the political situation, Stalin enumerated the aims of the Party in the international revolutionary movement. Three of these aims, he said, had already won general recognition. They were: (1) the strengthening of the communist parties in western countries and the winning over of the masses to the cause of communism; (2) the bringing about of a closer coöperation between the trade unions in capitalist countries and in the U. S. S. R. and the united front of labor; (3) a closer collaboration between the U. S. S. R. and the movements for national liberation in oppressed countries. To these three generally recognized purposes Stalin added a fourth, the victory of the socialist over the capitalist elements in the Union itself and the establishing of socialism in Russia as a factor of decisive values in revolutionizing the workers of other countries. While speaking of the policies to be followed for the stimulation of the world revolutionary movement, Stalin pointed out that one very often overlooked the fact that the struggle being carried on in

[34] *Ibid.*, pp. 673–674.

Russia "for the victory of the socialist over the capitalist elements, the struggle for the constructive, is in its essence an international struggle, because our country is the foundation of the international revolution, because it is the chief motive power in the development of the international revolutionary movement, and if we are making here satisfactory progress, this means that we are also performing our work in all the other phases of the international revolutionary movement in accordance with the requirements of the Party." [35]

In 1926, as we have seen, Stalin had no longer any ground to complain that the importance of the achievements of socialism in the U. S. S. R., from the point of view of world revolution, had been overlooked. With the final defeat of the Opposition and the exile of Trotsky, the doctrine of socialism in a single country had not only been officially accepted, but had also been put vigorously into practice.

Fortunately, it is unnecessary for us to decide which of the two opposing sections of the Communist Party was right in interpreting Lenin. It would certainly seem that Trotsky and his friends had a case which at least deserved serious consideration. On the other hand, Stalin's doctrine had obvious and important advantages in making possible the pursuance of a clear-cut and vigorous domestic policy, and the seeking of a *modus vivendi* with the

[35] *Chetirnadtsati Sezd Vsesoyuznoi Kommunisticheskoi Partii (Fourteenth Congress of the Communist Party of the Soviet Union),* December 18–31, 1925, verbatim report, Moscow—Leningrad, 1926, p. 26.

outside world, which might well be worth some rather questionable departure from not only the letter, but also the spirit, of the teaching of Marx, Engels, and Lenin. But, as we know, Stalin would never admit that such departures were being made. Whatever may be the theoretical weaknesses of the new communist theory, its practical effects are unmistakable. It brought to an end a situation which, according to Stalin, existed in Russia in 1923, on the eve of the revolutionary outbreak in Germany, when young communists were only too anxious to abandon their studies and their work in Moscow and run to Berlin on the assumption that, as revolutionaries had nothing more to do in Russia, their place was on the barricades of the German capital. Such an attitude was now officially declared to be "counter-revolutionary opportunism." The Soviet Union was on the point of embarking upon the most ambitious scheme of industrialization and economic reconstruction the world had ever seen. The theoretical justification for this great undertaking was laid down in Stalin's new doctrine.

CHAPTER V

INTERNATIONAL IMPLICATIONS OF THE NEW DOCTRINE

IMMEDIATE INFERENCES

THE official adoption of "socialism in a single country" as orthodox Leninist doctrine offered the Russian Communist Party a way out of the tragic *impasse* into which it had been forced by the failure of world revolution to materialize. The recognition of a period of stabilized capitalism coincided with the acceptance of Stalin's theory. The fifth congress of the Comintern in 1924 still insisted that an immediate struggle between capital and the proletariat was imminent, but in 1925 it was officially admitted that the capitalist world had entered upon a period of provisional stabilization.[1] The Soviet leaders could now face the temporary shelving of world revolution with a certain composure, because they were confronted with a stupendous task at home which, as we know, was also construed as meaning the advancement of the ultimate aim of communism. The Five Year Plan was already looming on the horizon and was soon to centre the attention of the nation.

[1] Verbatim report of the fourteenth congress of the Communist Party of the Soviet Union, December 18–31, 1925, pp. 10, 957.

The advantages of a planned economy over the "anarchy of production" which prevails in the world of capitalism and inevitably leads to crises of overproduction and depression is one of the generally accepted and integral postulates of Marxian teaching. It was naturally out of the question to apply it in practice in the Soviet Union while it was at war with the White armies and the capitalist countries. With the adoption of the New Economic Policy in 1921 and the resumption of more or less normal relations with other nations, a notable improvement took place in both the domestic and international position of the Union. It was perfectly proper, therefore, that the Soviet Government should turn at once to the laying down of a framework for state economic planning. The establishment of the Gosplan or State Planning Commission went back to 1921.[2] At the beginning, however, this much advertised institution played a relatively unimportant part, and it was only after the official acceptance of socialism in a single country that it immensely expanded the scope of its work. In 1925 it published its first "control figures"; and in 1926 was launched the Five Year Plan, revised in 1927, which is justly considered one of the outstanding developments in the crowded history of the whole post-war period. It was an economic experiment which, undoubtedly, was made possible only by the ending of the civil war, the Allies' abandonment of

[2] A still earlier planning body, the State Electrification Commission, had been appointed a year before, in February, 1920.

the Russian blockade, and the economic revival which followed the adoption of the New Economic Policy.

But none of these conditions, however important and significant in themselves, would have sufficed to explain the new and stupendous venture upon which the Soviet Union embarked, if one did not take into account the Soviet Government's recently acquired confidence in the possibility of achieving the goal—that setting up of integral socialism within the Russian frontiers, irrespective of what was happening to the capitalist world outside. To repeat the assertion of Stalin, it was impossible to establish socialism if one did not have the sense of certainty that the task was a feasible one. Before asking the country to make innumerable and heavy sacrifices for the ultimate success of the great venture, the communist leaders had to convince themselves and their followers that these sacrifices would not be wasted, and that the gigantic enterprise they had undertaken had the blessing of the great revolutionary prophet, Lenin. We are already familiar with the somewhat questionable method by which this was achieved.

There was also a necessary and logical consequence of the new doctrine, with its practical expression, the Five Year Plan, and this was the shifting of the interest of the communist leaders from international to domestic problems. The speedy industrialization of Russia demanded closer coöperation with the more advanced countries, as had been admitted by Stalin as early as December, 1925. "In the field of international relations," he declared at the fourteenth congress of the Russian Communist Party, "we are confronted with the need of consolidating and developing what has been accomplished during the 'breathing space' which has grown into a whole period of so-called peaceful co-existence of the U.S.S.R. alongside the capitalist nations, in spite of the fact that the contradictions between the two camps tend not to decrease, but to increase. This offers guarantees for economic construction at home and, thanks to economic relations with countries abroad, means certain advantages for the speeding up of our economic construction. On the other hand, the growing ties between our economy and world capitalism add to our dependence on the latter, and create new dangers which the party must take into account in this work of economic reconstruction as also in that of safeguarding our country's vital economic independence."[3] This necessity for international economic coöperation raised a number of novel problems which it was not always easy to reconcile with the traditional methods of communism.

THE CHINESE REVOLUTION

It would be, of course, entirely wrong to imagine that the foreign policy of the Soviet Union underwent a sharp and sudden change as a result of the

[3] Verbatim report of the fourteenth congress of the Communist Party of the Soviet Union, p. 513.

modifications which had taken place in the teaching and domestic policies of the Moscow Government. The Eastern problem figured largely in the pre-occupations of the Soviet leaders in 1923–1927. The attempts to improve the relations of the U. S. S. R. with the European nations did not mean the abandonment of revolutionary activities. The defeats suffered by world revolution in the West naturally suggested seeking a more fertile field in the colonial and semi-colonial countries to which Lenin attached so much importance.

China, that traditional foothold of world imperialism, seemed to offer revolutionary propaganda elements which might set the whole East ablaze. Indeed, the conditions prevailing in China after the war seemingly gave communism a particularly suitable field for its subversive activities. Karakhan, the Soviet envoy to China, was busying himself there, in accordance with the plans of Moscow, with a considerable degree of success. In September, 1923, Michael Borodin came to Canton and soon became an important factor in Chinese politics. Moscow under the guidance of Stalin and the Comintern spared neither effort nor money to create a Chinese Soviet Republic. It was a policy that was bitterly attacked by the Opposition and by Trotsky, who laid the failure of the Chinese revolution at the door of its advisers from Moscow. We shall not attempt to go into the details of this controversy. It will be sufficient for our purpose to recall the fact that the communist revolution in China proved as abortive as it had been in western Europe. In the summer of 1927 Borodin was forced to return to Russia without having succeeded in fulfilling his ultimate purpose. The East, too, refused, at least for the time being, to follow Moscow's lead.

This was a new and a severe blow. It unquestionably strengthened the determination of the Soviet leaders to proceed with that program on which they had already embarked, the establishing of integral socialism in Russia.

THE SIXTH CONGRESS OF THE COMINTERN

There still remained the difficult and delicate task of fitting the policy of international economic co-operation, resulting from the program of industrialization, into the general forms of communist theory. This was performed to the satisfaction of Stalin and his friends by the sixth congress of the Comintern, which met in July–August, 1928. The preceding, or fifth, congress had been held in the summer of 1924. The ominous interval of four years which had thus elapsed between the fifth and sixth has never been officially explained. Trotsky suggested that it was due to the fact that the leaders of the Comintern were hoping against hope for some international development which could be interpreted as a proof of the wisdom of their general policy; a successful revolution in at least some colonial country, or a great strike which would indicate the approaching downfall of capitalism. We may, perhaps, venture the opinion that the delay in calling together the governing body of the world revolution was the result of the desire of Moscow to prevent further friction between the Soviet Union and capitalist countries, friction which would interfere with the development of trade relations with the outside world, on which the success of the industrialization program so largely depended. The activities of the Comintern were followed closely and with much suspicion by the capitalist Powers, especially since the unhappy publicity that had been given to the so-called "Zinoviev letter." Another possible reason for the delay might be found in the marked difficulties which arose in connection with the revision of some of the fundamental doctrines of communism, and in the preparation of the ambitious and, from the communist point of view, highly important document known as the Program of the Comintern. It incorporated the new theory of Stalin as an integral part of the body of communist international policy.

The sixth congress of the Comintern was entirely dominated by Stalin and Bukharin. Zinoviev and Trotsky, as well as a score of minor leaders of the Opposition, had already disappeared from the political stage. Officially, Bukharin was, perhaps, the leading figure of the sixth congress, but it was also in a sense to hear his swan song; for, as a member of the Right Opposition, which criticized what it believed to be the too extreme and intolerant policies of Stalin and his friends, he was soon to pass into oblivion.[4] But if, during the sixth congress, his

[4] In this connection it may be of interest to recall the prophetic statement made by Stalin at the fourteenth congress of the Rus-

position was not altogether secure, he was still largely responsible for the decisions of the international gathering that was to determine the future of the world revolutionary movement for years to come.

The sixth congress of the Comintern performed the momentous task of providing the international communist movement with a definite program, one which not only embodied the fundamental principles of communist teaching but also determined the general lines of the policy actually to be followed by the Comintern and the communist parties, a policy which, it was claimed, was built upon the firm foundation of an objective Marxian analysis of the proletarian struggle against the bourgeoisie, and, especially, upon the practical experiences of the revolutionary movement since 1917. The Program of the Communist International, in order to be fully understood, must be examined in connection with the "Theses and Resolutions" adopted by the sixth congress and dealing with the international situation, the struggle against imperialistic war, and the revolutionary movement in the colonies and

sian Communist Party in December, 1925. Criticizing the demand of Zinoviev and Kamenev, who at that time were bitterly opposing Trotsky, for his expulsion from the party, Stalin said, "We do not agree with comrades Zinoviev and Kamenev, because we know that the policy of 'cutting off' [errant members] is fraught with danger to the party, that the method of cutting off, the method of bleeding—and they do demand blood—is contagious; to-day we cut off one, to-morrow—another, the day after to-morrow—a third. But—by then, what will be left of the party?" (Verbatim report, p. 502.) Zinoviev and Kamenev later learned the truth of these words by bitter and personal experience.

semi-colonies, with special reference in every case to the task of the Comintern. It is by no means a simple and easy task to give, in a few pages, an adequate and comprehensive idea of these ambitious documents, which run into tens of thousands of words and claim the distinction of setting forth a logical and complete economic, political, social, and ethical system. It must be attempted, nevertheless, if we are to provide a general theoretical background for the understanding of the more recent attitude of the Soviet Union, especially in its relations with foreign nations.

THE PROGRAM OF THE COMINTERN

Until the sixth congress the Comintern had no codified program. It was using for its guidance the *Communist Manifesto* written in 1848 by Marx and Engels, and also the various manifestoes and resolutions issued by the earlier congresses of the Comintern. It is rather significant that some of the more important of these earlier documents, for instance the manifestoes issued by the first congress in 1919 and by the second congress in 1920, were written by Trotsky, who, during the sixth congress, was an exile. The desire for a complete and comprehensive statement of communist doctrine became plain during the first years of the Soviet régime, and the question was discussed at the fourth congress in 1922, when some of the national communist parties— those of Germany, Bulgaria, Italy, and Japan—submitted draft programs. The issue, however, was

shelved for the time being on the suggestion of
Lenin, who considered that it called for more careful
study. The draft accepted by the sixth congress was
prepared by a special committee, and was largely
the work of Stalin and Bukharin.

It would, of course, be idle to expect that an international communist organization such as the
Comintern could openly repudiate the teachings of
Marx, Engels, and Lenin, although, as we have seen,
the possibility of their partial revision could not be
excluded. The Program of the Comintern preserved
the whole of the revolutionary phraseology of the
Communist Manifesto; and from the point of view
of style and uncompromising expression it can stand
comparison with any of the documents issued by
earlier congresses which followed more directly upon
the revolution. But revolutionary phraseology may
cover a great many things, just as the teachings of
Christ proved by no means incompatible with the
atrocities of the Spanish Inquisition. We shall en-
deavor, therefore, to discover, under this cloak of
uncompromising revolutionary utterances, the real
meaning of the Program and its practical implications. And, before we proceed with the more important part of our task, a brief outline of the contents of the Program may be useful.

It was divided into six parts and an introduction.[5]

[5] We are using the English text of the Program which was
published as a part of the abbreviated proceedings of the Sixth
World Congress of the Communist International, as issued by
the *International Press Correspondence,* Vol. VIII, Nos. 39–92
(July 25–December 31, 1928), Vienna.

It opened with the statement that the epoch of imperialism is the epoch of moribund capitalism. The war of 1914–1918 and the crisis of capitalism which followed it are the direct results of the contradictions between the growth of the productive forces of the world and national state barriers. They have created an intolerable situation which can be remedied only by the forcible overthrow of capitalism, the time for which has fully arrived. Imperialism proceeds by methods of blood, iron, and starvation, thus forcing the proletariats of all races, nations, and languages to unite to overthrow their oppressors. Imperialism, therefore, not only creates the material prerequisites for socialism, but "at the same time it musters the army of its own gravediggers": it forces the proletariat to organize itself in the Third Communist International, a militant association of all peoples enlisted for the destruction of imperialism. "The Program of the Communist International, being the supreme critical generalization of the whole body of historical experience of the international revolutionary proletarian movement, becomes the program of struggle for the world proletarian dictatorship, the program of struggle for world communism." The Communist International stands on the platform of "revolutionary Marxism and its further development, Leninism, which is nothing else but Marxism of the epoch of imperialism and proletarian revolutions." It is uncompromisingly opposed to any doctrine of class collaboration, and is the only international force which has for its program the dictatorship of the proletariat and that openly comes out as the organizer of the international proletarian revolution.

After this ominous introduction came Part I, entitled "The World System of Capitalism, Its Development and Inevitable Downfall." It began with a brief summary of the familiar Marxian analysis of the epoch of industrial capitalism: the evils of private ownership of the means of production; the exploitation of the wage earners; the anarchy of production with the resulting general overproduction and recurrent crises accompanied by mass unemployment; the concentration and centralization of capital and the crowding out of small producers, due largely to technical progress and the advantages of large-scale production; the growing dependence of the worker on the capitalist, resulting in the ruthless exploitation of the proletariat and the increased employment of female and child labor; the formation of enormous reserve armies of labor; and the creation of two irreconcilably opposed social groups, a small group of degenerate capitalists on one side, and a constantly growing mass of destitute and exploited labor on the other. The period of industrial capitalism, generally speaking, is a period of free competition, of the expansion of capitalism throughout the world, of the building of colonial empires at the expense of the less advanced nations in overseas territories not yet occupied by other capitalist powers.

The first years of the twentieth century saw the

beginning of the era of imperialism or financial capitalism, an era characterized by the merging of industrial capital with bank capital, and the transformation of the former era of free competition into one dominated by a monopoly of financial capital. Competition, nevertheless, has not been eliminated but has been carried on on a much vaster scale by gigantic financial combinations. This competition and the decline in the rate of profits resultant upon the necessity of making huge investments in expensive machinery and producing on a continuously increasing scale has created an insatiable demand for new markets. It has been accompanied by a rapid increase in foreign investments, and a struggle for the possession of fuel and raw materials coming from the most distant corners of the earth. All these conditions have inevitably led to a struggle among the imperialistic nations for a redivision of a world which they had already divided. This struggle might take the form of boycotts, or of high protective tariffs, but it inescapably results in imperialistic wars. The development of imperialism has brought the masses of the proletariat into sharp conflict not only with their employers but also with the capitalist state as a whole; it has also created conflicts between the capitalist states and the population of the colonies; and, finally, between the capitalist states themselves. Imperialism has reproduced the contradictions of industrial capitalism on a larger scale. It has also completed the work of its predecessor in preparing the world for socialism by greatly developing its productive forces. Imperialistic wars, which can only grow into world wars, have placed an intolerable burden upon the shoulders of the proletariat and demonstrated the degeneracy of the whole system. Monopolistic producers have also shown a tendency to slow down the development of the productive forces by a policy of cartel prices. The possibility of an "organized" capitalism advocated by the Social Democrats is a mere illusion. They can do nothing to soften the antagonisms from which the world is suffering under imperialism. "It is the final stage of the development of the capitalist system. It is the threshold of world social revolution." It is now approaching its doom and is about to give way to the dictatorship of the proletariat.

Having thus established the theoretical inevitability of the impending collapse of capitalism, the Program proceeded to examine its application in practice. This it did in Part II, which dealt with "The General Crisis of Capitalism and the First Phase of World Revolution." The war of 1914–1918, described as the first imperialistic war, resulted from the struggle among the capitalist states for the redistribution of the globe. It shook the whole mechanism of imperialism and, inevitably, led to the intensification of the class struggle and to civil war. So far, however, the latter has been successful in Russia alone. Revolutionary outbreaks in other countries have been defeated because of the predatory and treasonable policies of the labor leaders. The

Social Democrats and Fascism are two of the worst enemies of the proletariat and world revolution. The stabilization of capitalism in the post-war world is, however, purely transitory. As a result of the first clash of imperialistic wars the world has now been split into two hostile camps: that of the imperialist states and that of the dictatorship of the proletariat in the U. S. S. R. Two irreconcilably antagonistic systems are now facing each other: capitalism and socialism. It is only since the proletariat has, in Russia, acquired a permanent base that the proletarian struggle has been really carried on on a world scale. "The existence of the Soviet Union and the influence it exercises upon the toiling and oppressed masses all over the world is in itself a most striking expression of the profound crisis in the world capitalist system, and of the expansion and intensification of the class struggle to a degree hitherto without parallel in history." The contradictions within the capitalist system in the meantime are growing more and more pronounced. Foremost among them is the shifting of the economic centre of the world to the United States; and to add to this, the fact that "the Dollar Republic has become a world exploiter has caused the relations between the United States and European capitalism, primarily British capitalism, to become strained." The impending conflict between the United States and Great Britain is one of primary importance. There is also the conflict between Germany and the former Allies; and likewise the conflict between the

United States and Japan. The withdrawal of the Soviet Union, with its large reserves of mineral fuel and raw materials, from the close circle of imperialistic monopolies has accentuated the struggle among the capitalist nations. There is also an intensification of the hostility of the colonial nations to their foreign oppressors, and between capital and labor—labor being driven into revolutionary channels by concerted attacks on its organizations, political rights, and standards of living. All these conditions —conflicts between capitalist states, disaffection in the colonies, growing discontent among the workers at home, and the revolutionary influence of the Soviet Union—together menace the imperfect stabilization of capitalism. The world revolution is drawing near. "Against this revolution imperialism is gathering its forces. Expeditions against the colonies, a new world war, a campaign against the U. S. S. R., are matters which now figure prominently in the policies of imperialism. This must lead to the release of all forces of international revolution and to the inevitable doom of capitalism."

Part III dealt briefly with "The Ultimate Aim of the Communist International—World Communism," and it is to rid us of class divisions in society, private ownership of the means of production, exploitation of man by man, and finally of the state itself. The higher form of communist commonwealth will carry into practice the principle, "From each according to his abilities, to each according to his needs." But before this stage is reached the world must pass through the lower form of organization, that of the socialist society which is not completely free from all the contradictions from which capitalism is suffering.

Part IV went into "The Period of Transition from Capitalism to Socialism and the Dictatorship of the Proletariat." The period of transition from the world dictatorship of imperialism to the world dictatorship of the proletariat is to be one of many years, years filled with crises, wars, internal struggles, and periods of relative peace. The law of uneven development of capitalism, so particularly pronounced during the era of imperialism, excludes the possibility of any revolution that will be simultaneous in all countries. Socialism will win at first in one or a few countries, and thus broaden the basis for the world revolution. The conquest of power by the proletariat and the establishment of a dictatorship is a necessary preliminary to the complete achievement of socialism. The characteristic feature of this period will be the ruthless suppression of all resistance by the capitalists and the gradual elimination of class society. The dictatorship of the proletariat cannot be established by peaceful means such as the winning of parliamentary majorities. The rule of the bourgeoisie is based on force and it can be overthrown only by irresistible severity on the part of the proletariat. It must destroy the controlling mechanisms of the bourgeois state and replace them by the new mechanisms of the proletarian government.

That new form of state, the one which has grown

out of the Russian revolution of 1917 and the revolution in Hungary, is the Soviet state. It is the highest form of proletarian democracy, and it is the very opposite of bourgeois democracy. The Soviet state is the dictatorship of one class, the proletariat, and this it openly admits, while under the democratic régime the bourgeoisie seeks to disguise its dictatorship behind the veil of illusory class coöperation. The seizure of power by the proletariat is a necessary step, preliminary to the carrying out of the economic revolution, the process of expropriating from the expropriators, the turning of what has been the monopolistic property of the bourgeoisie into the property of the proletarian state. The exact nature of the economic policy of the proletariat must be determined by the relationship between the classes in each several country. The regular conditions of buying and selling will be maintained at the beginning; and it will be incumbent on the dictatorship to strike the proper balance between the various producers, from the great state-controlled industries to the small peasant farmers. But the technical superiority of extensive socialized industries and of large-scale coöperative farming must tend wholly to eliminate private enterprise with the result that marketing, in its ordinary meaning, will gradually disappear. "War Communism," while justified by the necessities of the struggle for power, can not be regarded as the normal economic policy of the proletarian dictatorship.

Under the dictatorship of the proletariat the class

struggle still goes on, although under new conditions. The use of force is necessary to stamp out the last remains of bourgeois society. While ruthlessly eliminating the former upper classes, the proletariat must win over a section of the skilled-artisan intelligentsia, and especially the mass of the "poor" and "middle" peasants. While the leadership of the proletarian dictatorship belongs to the industrial workers, it must be based on their alliance with the peasantry. Here an important rôle is played by the mass organizations of labor, which turned into institutions for the education of the masses in the ideas of communism. A similar part is played, in the villages, by the coöperative societies. But the leading place under the proletarian dictatorship must be held by the Communist Party, which assures the Soviet Government of that support of the masses without which it could not exist. Accompanying the economic and political revolution, there is also a cultural revolution, which has for its goal the final removal of class society and a complete change in human nature. Among the evil forces of capitalism which are to be eliminated is religion, the opium of the people.

The international proletarian revolution will proceed by slow stages, and in these various stages there will be purely proletarian revolutions, revolutions of a bourgeois-democratic type which will develop into proletarian revolutions; wars for national emancipation, and colonial revolutions. The world dictatorship of the proletariat is the final stage of this revolutionary process. From the point of view of their readiness for revolution the countries of the world fall into three groups: (1) those of a highly developed capitalism, such as the United States, Germany, and Great Britain, which are fully ripe for the dictatorship of the proletariat; (2) countries with a halfway development of capitalism, such as Poland, Portugal, Hungary, and the Balkan States, which still retain semi-feudal conditions in their agriculture, and where the establishment of the proletarian dictatorship largely depends on winning over the peasantry; (3) "colonial and semi-colonial" countries, such as China and India, and "dependent" countries, such as Argentina and Brazil, which are generally speaking, not yet ripe for socialism; in these countries the task of communism consists very largely in organizing agrarian revolutions and struggles against foreign oppressors. The dictatorship of the proletariat in such countries can be established only by slow degrees and with the support of countries where the proletariat has already won a victory. In the still more backward countries such as certain parts of Africa, where there is practically no native bourgeoisie, the proletarian struggle must be concentrated and express itself in the denunciation of foreigners and in conflicts for national independence. With the assistance of countries controlled by the dictatorship of the proletariat, the backward nations when on their way to socialism might altogether avoid the capitalistic stage. This greatly emphasizes the importance of the U. S. S. R. as a leading factor in world revolution. Colonial revolutions and movements for national emancipation are extremely important in the struggle against imperialism. The relations between industrial and colonial countries are somewhat similar to those between the industrial proletariat and the peasantry; colonial countries are "world villages," while the industrial countries are "world cities." A solid militant alliance between them, therefore, is of tremendous importance during the transition period.

Part V of the Program treated of "The Dictatorship of the Proletariat in the International Social Revolution"; that is, it concerned itself with the U. S. S. R. as a factor in world revolution. The most striking evidence of the crisis of capitalism is the division of the post-war world into two groups of nations; the capitalist nations and those engaged in the building of socialism. "The internal consolidation of the proletarian dictatorship in the U. S. S. R., the success achieved in the work of socialist construction, the growth of the influence and authority of the U. S. S. R. among the masses of the proletariat and the oppressed peoples of the colonies mean, accordingly, the continuation, intensification, and expansion of the international social revolution." The policy of the Russian Communist Party during the first ten years of the dictatorship has been fully vindicated by the results achieved, and the country is now well on its way toward the setting up of integral socialism which, it knows, can be established within national frontiers in spite of the obstacles presented by technical and economic backwardness. As the

only country under the dictatorship of the proletariat, the Soviet Union inevitably becomes the basis
for the world movement of the oppressed classes,
the centre of the international revolution, and, as
such, the dominating factor in the history of the
world. The U.S.S.R. is of vast importance as
being the world's great revolutionary power; it is
the international driving force of world revolution,
the living example which proves that the working
class is not only capable of seizing power, but also
of achieving socialism; it is the precursor of the
world union of the socialist republics of the future.
This immense importance of the Soviet Union imposes upon its government the duty of fighting for
its existence, and of safeguarding the interests of
the proletarian state by means of "economic manœu-
vring." Its economic policy is based on the expansion of its economic relations with capitalist
countries so long as they serve the purposes of
socialist construction. Only by making the Union
economically independent and self-sufficient is it
possible to put the great work of establishing socialism on a firm foundation and remove the danger of
seeing the U.S.S.R. transformed into a mere satellite of the capitalist nations. In spite of their interest in trading with Russia, the capitalist nations are
fully aware of her importance as the centre of world
revolution; and the general tendency of their policy
is to encircle the U.S.S.R., with a view to strangling it and establishing a world régime of bourgeois terrorism. But, nevertheless, this ever-present

danger does not prevent the Soviet state from fulfilling its mission of rendering all possible assistance to the exploited and the oppressed in all parts of the world in their struggle against the bourgeoisie.

This position of the Soviet Union also imposes definite obligations upon the international proletariat. It is its duty to defend the Union against the attacks of the capitalist nations by all means at its disposal. This applies to both the workers in the advanced countries and to the native population in the colonies. The progress of socialism in the U. S. S. R. and the growth of its international influence not only foments the hatred of the capitalist states and their Social Democratic agents, but also inspires the workers of the world with enthusiasm and admiration for the U. S. S. R.'s achievements and stimulates their determination to defend it from attacks from the outside. This, again, intensifies antagonisms in the capitalist world and paves the way for revolutionary outbreaks which will spell the doom of capitalism.

The sixth and last section of the Program outlined "The Strategy and Tactics of the Communist International in the Struggle for the Dictatorship of the Proletariat." It opened with a bitter denunciation of all non-communist movements among the working classes such as Social Democracy, the Amsterdam International, His Britannic Majesty's socialists of the British Labor Party, Fabianism, the "coöperative" socialism of Charles Gide, the "guild" social-

ism of Hobson and Orage, the Austro-Marxism, anarchism, revolutionary syndicalism, and the national
radical movements; for example, those of Sun Yat-
sen, Gandhi, and Garvey. All alike, such movements
are branded as treason to the real cause of the
working classes, whose only real representative is
proletarian communism. The communist strategy
and tactics in the advanced countries are determined in accordance with the principles laid down by
the earlier congresses of the Comintern: the struggle
for the control of the masses, the support of every
movement for emancipation in the colonies, the policy of a "single labor front," and the winning over
to communism of the trade unions. The Comintern
must concern itself especially with the struggle
against imperialistic wars. It must denounce the
bourgeois pacifist organizations, especially those of
the Social Democrats, which seek to minimize the
danger; to engage in propaganda in favor of the ideas
of the Comintern, especially propaganda in the armies of the capitalist states. The fundamental principles which must determine this work are these:
to convert imperialistic war into civil war; to defeat the imperialistic governments at home; and
to defend the U.S.S.R. and the colonial countries in the event of a war against them. It is
particularly important to reveal the imperialistic
schemes devised by the capitalistic nations under
cover of the League of Nations.

The Program appropriately closed with the celebrated paragraph from the *Communist Manifesto* of

1848: "The communists disdain to conceal their views and aims. They openly declare that their goal can be attained only by the forcible overthrow of all existing social conditions. Let the ruling class tremble before the communist revolution. The proletarians have nothing to lose but their chains. They have a world to win. Workers of all countries, unite!"

THE PROGRAM ANALYZED

This brief summary of the Program may suffice to indicate its general trend and argument. It will be readily admitted that it contains enough revolutionary phraseology to send thrills of horror down the spinal columns of the timorous spinsters of both sexes and of all weak-kneed statesmen who believe that the plague of communism can be imported and disseminated like a contagious disease, that a nation or a part of it can be infected with Bolshevism as if Bolshevism were typhus or scarlet fever. The Program, as we have seen, simply bristles with the inevitable downfall of capitalism, and with pledges, seemingly unqualified, of the Soviet's support of the cause of world revolution. A closer examination of the Program may lead us to a somewhat different conclusion.

It is not our purpose to pass upon the general validity of this communist analysis of the period of industrial capitalism and imperialism, although we may venture the opinion that it added little to the lustre of Marxian dialectics, if Marxian dialectics found expression in it. Trotsky has described the policy of Stalin and Bukharin embodied in the Program as "a blind empiricism multiplied by scholastics."[6] Trotsky, of course, had never sinned on the side of excessive objectivity or impartiality, and his judgments on Stalin must be naturally taken with a grain of salt. But he is a faithful soldier of the world revolution and his opinion on the Program of the Comintern is not without interest.

He compared the Program to a ship which was equipped and even overloaded with all sorts of modern (Marxian) instruments and appliances, but the mainsail of which had purposely been flung wide to all the winds of "reformism and opportunism."[7] Under such conditions it was the winds, of course, and not the vessel's elaborate instruments which determined her course. The conspicuous weakness of the Program, irrespective of the general validity of the Marxian or quasi-Marxian analysis, is the irreconcilable contradiction between its fundamental proposition that the international economic interdependence of the world is incompatible with national political barriers and inevitably lead to the collapse of the capitalist system,—and Stalin's doctrine of socialism in a single country. It is difficult to see, and the Program certainly did nothing to clear up this point, why the economic interdependence of the world, which spelled the doom of capitalism, should suddenly lose its destructive power when

[6] Léon Trotsky, *L'internationale communiste après Lénine*, p. 221.

[7] *Ibid.*, p. 116.

applied to a country which had adopted a Soviet form of government. The truly revolutionary departure of the Program from the pronouncements of the Comintern in the past lies in the emphasis it puts on the Soviet Union as a factor in world revolution. It will be remembered that the Program declared that the consolidation of the proletarian dictatorship in the U. S. S. R., the success achieved in the work of socialist construction, and the growth of its influence among the masses meant "the continuation, intensification, and expansion of the international social revolution"; that it was the duty of the Soviet Government to enter into close relations with the capitalist nations in order to insure the success of its work of reconstruction; and that it was the duty of the international proletariat to defend the U. S. S. R. by all means at its disposal. Obviously the celebrated phrases of the *Communist Manifesto,* "The proletarians have nothing to lose but their chains. They have a world to win," did not apply to the Russian proletariat. They had alread broken their chains and gained the guerdon,— within their own national frontiers, at any rate,— irrespective of what might be the fate of the world revolution. The difference between the policies to be followed within the Soviet Union and in the capitalist nations had been clearly stated by Varga in an elaborate report to the sixth congress of the Comintern on the economic situation in the U. S. S. R. "In the capitalist countries the proletariat fights against the capitalist state," he said; "in the

U. S. S. R. the proletariat defends its government, it defends the proletarian state. In the capitalist countries we are for revolution; in the U. S. S. R. we are for evolution, for internal peace, for the peaceful development of socialism. In the capitalist countries we are for the destruction of the capitalist system; in the Soviet Union we are working for the transformation of a class society into a socialist society, and eventually into a communist society. In the capitalist countries we are strongly opposed to any coöperation among the classes; in the U. S. S. R., on the contrary, we are for class coöperation; and an alliance between the proletariat and the masses of the toiling peasants forms the very foundation of the proletarian dictatorship in the Soviet Union." [8]

While reading the Program one might well infer that the all-powerful law of the economic interdependence of the world, on which the whole analysis is ostentatiously based, ceased to operate, as if by the touch of a magic wand, the moment Stalin and Bukharin turned their attention to the Soviet Union. The Program declared that the era of effective and solid socialist progress would come only after the proletariat was victorious throughout the whole world, and after it had consolidated its power. If this victory was to be interpreted in the sense in which it was understood now with reference to the Soviet Union, then, as Trotsky pointed out, [9] the world so-

[8] *Shestoi Kongress Kommunisticheskago Internatsionala (Sixth Congress of the Communist International)*, verbatim report, Moscow—Leningrad, 1929, Vol. V, p. 4.
[9] Léon Trotsky, *L'internationale communiste après Lénine*, p. 148.

cialism of the future would be built of "ready-made" national socialism, just as a child builds a castle of wooden blocks. In their enthusiasm for the Five Year Plan the authors of the Program seemed to have overlooked or forgotten the great principle of the international division of labor. This criticism, however, was anticipated at the sixth congress by Manuilsky, who discussed the immense difficulties which had been experienced by Russia in her economic reconstruction, as a result of an absence of real coöperation with the outside world. The "national self-sufficiency" of the U. S. S. R. which was so bitterly criticized by the opposition, Manuilsky declared, was forced upon it. "We are fully aware," he said, "that the victory of the proletariat in other capitalist countries will force us to rebuild our economy on the basis of the international division of labor." [10] This point of view, however, found no expression in the Program, nor is it among the slogans used by the Soviet leaders to promote industrialization, presumably because it would be of doubtful value in substantiating their claim of the significance of their achievements in advancing world revolution; nor would it be very helpful in calling upon the nation for further exertions and sacrifices.

IMPERIALISTIC WARS

We have already mentioned the important place occupied in the policies of the Soviet Union and the Comintern by the question of imperialistic war.

[10] Verbatim report of the sixth congress of the Communist International, Vol. V, p. 63.

Here, again, the new doctrine of Stalin led the communists into theoretical difficulties which are not easy to solve. The inevitability of imperialistic wars as a result of the antagonisms which exist under capitalism is emphasized over and over again in the Program and the Resolutions of the sixth congress. So long, then, as imperialistic wars were inevitable and were likely to be transformed first into civil wars and then into revolutions, one might be justified in assuming that the Comintern must welcome them. They would seem to offer the shortest road to world revolution. This, however, as we know, was exactly what the Comintern refused to do. The discussion of this question occupied a considerable part of the time of the sixth congress of the Comintern and its results were embodied in the lengthy document mentioned above, called "Thesis and Resolutions" dealing with "The Struggle against Imperialistic Wars and the Task of the Communists," and it was a document which considerably amplified the statements made in the Program. The real cause of wars, declared the Comintern, was, of course, not the evil nature of human beings, nor the bad policies followed by governments. It was the division of society into classes, into exploiters and exploited. Capitalism was the cause of war in modern society. Although wars were inevitable under capitalism, the U. S. S. R. was all for peace. Such a policy, it declared, was in the interest of the Russian and the international proletariat; for their aim was to safeguard international revolution and to protect the upbuilding of socialism in the Soviet Union. It implied strenuous opposition to all imperialistic wars, including those in the colonies, and the unmasking of bourgeois pacifism which was nothing else than a convenient camouflage for the plans of the imperialists. This policy of the Soviet Union, however, was not to be interpreted as meaning a reconciliation with capitalism, as had often been claimed by the Social Democrats and by Trotsky. It was described as merely another and, under existing conditions, a more advantageous method of fighting capitalism. But as the Russian proletariat has no illusions as to the inevitability of that war which was to be forced upon the Soviet Union by the capitalist nations, it must prepare for it by taking all necessary measures. "There is a glaring contradiction between the imperialists' policy of piling up armaments and their hypocritical talk about peace. There is no such contradiction, however, between the Soviet Government's preparations for defense and revolutionary war, and a consistent peace policy. Revolutionary war waged by the proletarian dictatorship is but a continuation of its revolutionary peace policy, 'by other means.'" It must be admitted that this is rather confused, and not very convincing. But the alarm about the impending "necessary and inevitable" attack upon the Soviet Union by the imperialistic powers sounded by the congress and the duty to defend the Soviet Union which such a threat imposed upon the proletariat of the world are reasonably clear, and within the grasp even of those who are not communists. The abhorrence of war which has grown up in the Soviet Union, especially since 1925, may be in contradiction to one of the fundamental ideas of communism; namely, that war is inevitable, and leads to civil war and to revolution. But it is a necessary part and element in Stalin's socialism in a single country. As Bell, the British delegate, put it at the sixth congress, "the Soviet Union, which has no territorial ambitions and is absorbed by the task of its economic socialist reconstruction, needs peace as one needs air, it needs it for the growth and development of the proletarian state." [11] And this is a task which, for the time being, has in the preoccupations of the Soviet leaders eclipsed and obscured their former interest in immediate world revolution.

The irreconcilable contradiction between the inevitability of war under capitalism and the determination of the U.S.S.R. to avoid it (in spite of the advantages which, according to the Program, an imperialistic war offers for the advancement of world revolution) has never been, to the best of our knowledge, satisfactorily explained by Soviet writers and statesmen, unless we are prepared to accept the statement already quoted above that the "revolutionary war waged by the proletarian dictatorship is but a continuation of its revolutionary peace policy, 'by other means.'" We must confess that the real meaning of this mysterious sentence is outside our

[11] Verbatim report of the sixth congress of the Communist International, Vol. II. p. 24.

grasp, which may be due to our unfamiliarity with Marxian dialectics. But then, as we know, according to Lenin, Bukharin himself, who is largely responsible for the work of the sixth congress, also never properly understood them.

Whatever may be the theoretical weaknesses of the anti-war policy of the U. S. S. R., its practical importance is unquestionable. Although war talks are kept permanently on the front pages of the Soviet newspapers, and the rattling of tanks and guns passing the tomb of Lenin in the Red Square is felt with apprehension by the timid souls outside the Union's borders, the policy of Moscow, so far, as will appear from our last chapter, has been distinctly in the direction of preventing a new war. And already we know the reason: the U. S. S. R. needs peace, as one needs air, in order to establish socialism within its national frontiers.

"THE THIRD PERIOD"

The same concern with the safeguarding of socialism in the U. S. S. R. is reflected in the much quoted "Theses" of the sixth congress on the international situation. We have already pointed out that the Soviet leaders have a strong liking for neat and well-organized historical systems. This is much in evidence in the Theses to which we are now referring. According to them, since the war, the world had passed through several periods, in which there could be seen the various phases of the decline of the capitalist system. The first period was a period of most acute crisis and was characterized by open, revolutionary struggle. It reached its highest point in 1921, and led, on the one hand, to the defeat of intervention in Russia, the consolidation of the Soviet rule, and the organization of the Communist International, and, on the other, to the defeat of the western proletariat by the capitalists. It closed with the failure of the revolutionary outbreaks in Germany in 1923. This defeat marked the beginning of the second period, which was characterized by the gradual and partial stabilization of capitalism and by speedy economic rehabilitation and restoration in the U. S. S. R. The third period, that of the present, has for its distinctive feature the fact that the level of economic development in both the capitalist world and the Soviet Union exceeds that of pre-war days. The rapid economic progress of the capitalist nations has been accompanied by an accentuation of internal contradictions, due to the disproportion between growing productive capacity and shrinking markets, the existence of the U. S. S. R., and so on. This third period must lead inevitably to a series of wars—wars among the imperialist states, wars against the U. S. S. R., wars for national liberation, and class conflicts on a gigantic scale. The intensification of international antagonisms— that between the capitalist world and the U. S. S. R. being a first example—and of internal antagonisms such as the growing acuteness of the class struggle, together with the development of colonial movements, inevitably result in the weakening of capital-

ist stabilization and in emphasizing the general crisis
of capitalism. In short, the third period means the
approaching end of capitalist stabilization and the
imminence of new revolutionary battles. This is
used as another occasion to underline the importance
of the reconstruction of the U. S. S. R. as an international revolutionary factor.

The "third period" has been bitterly criticized by
the Opposition and by Trotsky, who calls it "the
third period of the mistakes of the Comintern." They
maintain that there is not the slightest reason for
declaring that the time of gigantic revolutionary
battles is actually approaching. They agree, of
course, that new crises and imperialistic wars are
inevitable, but Trotsky also points out that the
Comintern puts itself in the position of a man who,
day after day, forecasts the eclipse of the sun for
the day following. Even if the eclipse does finally
take place, few would consider the gentleman in
question a serious astonomer. The leaders of the
Comintern with their "third period" deserve just as
much confidence.[12] We are inclined to agree with
Trotsky, although his own forecasts proved, perhaps,
just as unfortunate. But dealing with future events,
especially on a world scale, is in any case a hazardous
business. From the point of view of the general
policy laid down by Stalin and Bukharin at the
sixth congress, the "third period" had the unquestionable advantage of stressing the immediate

[12] Léon Trotsky, La "troisième période" d'erreurs de l'International Communiste, Paris, 1930, p. 35.

character of the dangers which are menacing the U.S.S.R. and thus stimulating its sympathizers both at home and abroad to further exertions for the defense of the first country of proletarian dictatorship.

THE NATIONAL COMMUNIST PARTIES

It is a real mental relief for a non-communist reader, when ploughing his way through the voluminous reports of the proceedings of various Soviet bodies, to come across passages which for a moment come down from the abstruse heights of Marxian theory, put aside the uncontrollable economic and social forces which are leading capitalism to its inevitable doom, and consent to discuss the actual progress of the communist movement in its more accessible and humble manifestations. These practical and *terre à terre* interludes offer an interesting and instructive picture of the actual work done by the Comintern and its sections or national communist parties. And it is much to the credit of the communist leaders that they are frank and outspoken in their self-criticism and are just as willing to admit their practical mistakes and failures as they are uncompromising in the defense of their principles. The proceedings of the sixth congress offered ample evidence that there was room for much improvement in the organization and work of the communist parties. We shall quote a few samples of criticisms taken more or less at random. Vassilev, reporting on the progress of the International of Communist Youth, which is the training school for the communist leaders of the future, sadly admitted that it left much to be desired. Outside the frontiers of the U. S. S. R. the membership of this organization did not exceed 100,000, and even this figure, relatively insignificant, was subject to considerable fluctuation, and certainly did not show any continuous growth. One of the chief purposes of the organization—the introduction of its members into large industrial enterprises for the purpose of establishing in them communist "cells"—remained practically unfulfilled. At the end of 1927 only 16 per cent of the young communists worked in large factories and plants, while 84 per cent were employed in small workshops. The "fluidity" of their membership lists was also very marked indeed.[13] Bodemann, representing Switzerland, complained of the tendency of the central organs of the Comintern to treat the communist parties of the small countries as *quantités négligeables*. It was impossible to obtain an answer from the Executive Committee of the Comintern even on questions of the greatest urgency. "I have reached the conclusion," he said, "that the huge machinery of the Executive Committee is working merely to keep itself busy, and is practically out of touch with the political leaders of the Comintern." Most of the "literature" sent to the Swiss party from Moscow was either out of date or in such a form that it could not be used. Questionable methods of propaganda were also not in-

[13] Verbatim report of the sixth congress of the Communist International, Vol. I, pp. 121–127.

frequently indulged in. What, for instance, could be the impression in western Europe when to-day the leading publication of the Comintern printed in heavy type and on its front page a statement to the effect that rumors as to the deportation and exile of the members of the Opposition were figments of the imagination of a bourgeois correspondent, and to-morrow the same publication stated in an editorial that the members of the Opposition should be grateful for being merely deported to Siberia. In any case such methods must completely deprive the masses of all confidence in the communist press.[14]

A rather interesting picture of the unhappy condition of the communist party in one city of the United States, Springfield,[15] was given in a report by Vassilev. The Springfield branch once had thirty-six members. But by July, 1928, only sixteen were left. No one knew what had happened to the others. The social composition of the membership was as follows: four petty artisans, three truck drivers, one housewife, two metal workers, and several textile hands. The local organization of Young Communists had twelve members, including seven high-school boys. And Springfield was a town with an industrial population of several thousands. "I ask you," Vassilev demanded, "when the party organization is on a social basis represented by the one I have described, can it offer any real opposition to war? There is

[14] *Ibid.*, p. 131.
[15] The name of the state was not given, probably Massachusetts.

only one answer. No!" [16] It would seem that in the other communist parties the organization of the anti-war work was also quite unsatisfactory. The sixth congress declared in its Theses that such anti-war activity was "excessively abstract, schematic, and even shallow." [17] Some of the communist parties, no doubt, had better equipped and more solid organizations. But much was still to be done before they could be turned into those powerful tools that were to tear down capitalism and replace it by the dictatorship of the proletariat. These considerations, it seems reasonable to assume, were not altogether absent from the minds of the leaders of the Comintern when they centred their attention on the Russian revolution and its achievements.

THE COMINTERN

The long road which the Communist International had travelled since its exuberant days of 1919 and 1920 is clearly shown by the definition of the immediate purpose of the communist movement given by the sixth congress. They were summarized as follows: the combating of the approaching imperialistic war, the defense of the U.S.S.R., the struggle against foreign intervention in China and her partition, the defense of the Chinese revolution and of colonial uprisings.[18] Among these aims, the defense of the U.S.S.R. came first. A victory of the im-

[16] Verbatim report of the sixth congress of the Communist International, Vol. II, p. 133.
[17] Theses on The Struggle against Imperialistic War, article 67.
[18] These on the International Situation, article 30.

perialists over the Soviet Union, the congress declared, would be much more than the defeat of the
Russian proletariat: it would also be the severest
defeat the international labor movement had ever
suffered. It would lead to an unprecedented victory
for reaction and for White terror throughout the
world. "It is essential, therefore, that attention
should be concentrated on the defense of the
U.S.S.R. Alarm for the fate of the U.S.S.R., which
is menaced by the gathering forces of imperialism,
must stimulate a coördinated work for the transformation of a war against the U.S.S.R. into a civil war
against the imperialistic governments, into a war
for the defense of the U.S.S.R." [19] Such was now
the chief immediate purpose of the Comintern. It
seems clear that in spite of all the revolutionary
phraseology of its Program and Resolutions the
Comintern had itself largely degenerated, or grown,
from the militant and uncompromising general staff
of the world revolution into an international organization for the defense of the U.S.S.R. The fact
that world revolution remained its ultimate goal
was, of course, undeniable. But unless one is a firm
believer in the unfailing wisdom of Marx, Engels,
and Lenin, and not only in their own wisdom, but
also in the correctness of the interpretation given
to their writings by Stalin and Bukharin—and the
latter had already been dropped by the Communist
Party—the ultimate goal of the Comintern is of
minor practical importance. What really matters is

[19] *Ibid.*, article 32.

the aim of the policy of the U. S. S. R. at the present time and in the reasonably near future. This policy was stated with sufficient clearness by the sixth congress of the Comintern. It was a policy that consisted in the prevention at any price of largely imaginary intervention in Russian affairs by the capitalist nations, and in a striving for the creation of a complete socialist state within Russian frontiers under the ægis of the Red army and the protection of the world proletariat. It remains for us to see whether this policy has actually been followed.

CHAPTER VI

TOWARD COOPERATION

THE FIRST STEPS

THE recognition of the primary importance of the Soviet Union's economic progress as a factor in world revolution and of the necessity for a *rapprochement* with the capitalist world, which were voiced by the sixth congress of the Third International, merely affixed the seal of official approval upon a policy already pursued for some time by the Moscow government. The importance of closer economic relations with the capitalist countries was, it will be remembered, admitted by the Bolshevik leaders as early as 1921 and was an essential corollary of the New Economic Policy. But it was only after the victory of Stalin over the Opposition, and the adoption of the vast program of industrialization, that the practical implications of the new doctrine began fully to be felt. Just as during the great struggle of 1914–1918 the slogan "All for the war" largely dominated the policies of the belligerent nations and often necessitated the discarding of deeply rooted political and social traditions and usages, so the slogan "All for industrialization" became the supreme principle to which all other considerations were subordinated. *Lex belli suprema lex.*

It called, as we have seen, for heavy personal sacrifices on the part of the population of the U. S. S. R.; and it also called for a revision of some of the fundamental ideas of the communist teaching. The industrialization policy of the Soviet Union has all the outward characteristics of a great national effort in a time of a military emergency. The terminology of the Russian Communist Party is that of a nation fighting for its existence. Soviet newspapers and books invariably speak of "mobilizations," "fronts," "offensives," "shock brigades," "strategic or tactical retreats," "victories," and so on. The devices for arousing national enthusiasm for the Five Year Plan and for keeping it alive are like those everywhere employed during the war. But all these quasi-military policies are here directed to an eminently peaceful purpose. The U. S. S. R. is a "nation in arms" struggling against its own backwardness and poverty for the establishment of integral socialism within its national frontiers. In this struggle it is only too anxious to enroll the support and assistance of the more advanced 'nations. The effects of this attitude upon the foreign policy of the Soviet Union are unmistakable. The foreign relations of the Union have consistently followed two chief lines: the development of economic ties between the U. S. S. R. and the capitalist nations, and the prevention of a new international war, the fear of which had grown into a virtual and, to a non-communist, a perfectly grotesque obsession. It seems doubtful whether the Soviet leaders themselves really believe in the danger of a war against the U. S. S. R. quite as much as they wish the country to think they do. But the danger of imperialistic aggression against the state of proletarian dictatorship serves a double purpose in the Soviet philosophy of to-day; it keeps alive the militant spirit of the Five Year Plan and it establishes a most useful link with the theory of world revolution, the complete abandonment of which no communist would ever concede.

It will be remembered that in 1921 the Soviet Union resumed trade relations with a number of European countries, that in 1924 it obtained *de jure* recognition from some of the leading governments, and that they were followed by other and minor powers. The year 1924 saw an interesting attempt to establish closer coöperation between the trade unions, in England and in the U. S. S. R. Negotiations were opened between the General Council of the English trade unions and the corresponding organization in the Soviet Union. An Anglo-Russian conference met in April, 1925, and this resulted in the creation of the Anglo-Russian Committee as the first step toward an alliance between Russian trade unions and those affiliated with the International Federation of Trade Unions (the Amsterdam International). The program of the Anglo-Russian Committee provided for a joint struggle against the advance of capital, the prevention of a new war, and joint action for the unification of the international labor movement. But coöperation between the Russian and English labor organizations proved anything but harmonious. Considerable friction developed when the English trade unions refused to accept Soviet aid for the striking miners of Great Britain; and they likewise refused to protect against the British policy in China (March, 1927), with the result that in September the whole project collapsed. The interesting feature of this short-lived development was the enthusiasm displayed in Moscow for this close collaboration with the British labor movement and the Amsterdam International which, it will be remembered, had always been denounced by the communists as their worst enemies. It was, no doubt, an attempt to realize on a large scale that "united front of labor" which had been one of the accepted principles of communism since the days of the third and fourth congresses of the Comintern; but it is perfectly clear that the "united front of labor" was not originally intended to include those labor leaders who were held responsible by the communists for the failure of the world revolutionary movement. What was really expected from the Anglo-Russian Committee was stated by Stalin at a meeting of the Executive Committee of the Central Control Committee, in July, 1926. "The task of the new 'bloc' [the Anglo-Russian Committee]," he said, "consists in the organization of a vast working class movement against new imperialistic wars in general, and especially against intervention in our country, as planned by the great European powers, particularly England." He then advanced the familiar argument that it was the duty of the international proletariat to defend the first republic of the workers against intervention and added: "If the reactionary British trade unions are willing to join with our revolutionary trade unions in an alliance against their own counterrevolutionary imperialists, then why should we not approve of the alliance?" Trotsky has pointed out, and we think rightly, that if Stalin really believed British trade unions to be reactionary, it was difficult to see why he expected them to fight against British imperialists. It would seem that he called his new British friends "reactionary" merely as a matter of habit, and actually entertained most extravagant illusions as to their revolutionary spirit.[1] Stalin's anxiety to provide a new guarantee against the expected intervention was, probably, an important consideration in turning the scale in favor of the ill-fated venture of the Anglo-Russian Committee.

ECONOMIC COLLABORATION

The general principles underlying the Soviet economic policy and attitude toward the capitalist world were clearly stated in a very significant resolution adopted by the fifteenth congress of the Russian Communist Party held in December, 1927. "The results of our economic development, following upon the inauguration of the so-called New Economic

[1] Léon Trotsky, *L'internationale communiste après Lénine*, p. 227.

Policy, which laid the foundations of the co-existence of socialized state industry with that of the small and the very small peasant producer, have fully confirmed the thesis of Lenin that we have in our country all the necessary elements for the establishing of socialism; that the objective internal conditions of the economic and social development of the U. S. S. R. contain no elements that make for its inevitable downfall, or for the disintegration of the dictatorship of the proletariat; and that the existence of a large number of peasant holdings, with collaboration between them and socialized institutions, does not necessarily limit our progress to that of a purely peasant country. . . . The experience of state planning has proved that our plans have required, not infrequently, revisions more or less considerable, that they are necessarily of a tentative and conditional character, that the real plan must inevitably develop organically and in harmony with an increasing degree of organization in the national economy and with the improvement in our methods of estimating and forecasting, consequent upon the growth of our socialized sector. . . . In planning our economic activities in the field of international relations, it is imperative to take as our point of departure not the bare consideration of a maximum development of such activities—such a principle, advanced by the Opposition, would, if applied logically, mean the abolition of the monopoly of foreign trade and an economic and military capitulation to the international bourgeoisie. It should not call for the restriction of our economic relations with the capitalist world. The application of this principle in practice would mean the slowing down of the tempo both of our economic progress and of that of the establishment of socialism in general. We must base our policy on the idea of a maximum development of our economic relations with foreign countries so far as such relations (expansion of foreign trade, foreign credits, concessions, employment of foreign technical advisers, etc.) contribute to the economic strength of the Union. We must make it more independent of the capitalist world, and broaden the socialist foundation for further industrial expansion of the Union. Only with these reservations can we speak of the maximum development of our economic relations." [2]

This policy of economic expediency, backed by the ideological propositions we have discussed, has been pretty consistently carried on by the Soviet Union in its relations with the capitalist world in the years that have followed the fifteenth congress of the Party. The former crusaders of world revolution at any cost have exchanged their swords for machine tools, and now rely more on the results of their labor than on direct action to achieve the ultimate victory of the proletariat.

The necessity of developing economic intercourse between the Soviet Union and the capitalist coun-

[2] *Pyatnadtsati Sezd Vsesoyuznoi Kommunisticheskoi Partii Bolshevikov (Fifteenth Congress of the Communist Party of the Soviet Union)*, verbatim report, Leningrad—Moscow, 1928, pp. 1291–1292.

tries became a favorite theme, one continuously discussed by Soviet statesmen and writers. Examining, for instance, the effect of industrialization and of the collectivization of farming upon Russo-German relations, the *Pravda,* the official organ of the Communist Party, said forcibly, "These developments are in no way harmful to German interests in the U. S. S. R. but, on the contrary, open a broader field for the expansion of Germany's economic activities in the Soviet Union. One must forget the time when the chimney stacks of German factories were belching smoke and Russia was merely an agricultural satellite. It is the desire of the U. S. S. R. that factory chimneys should pour out their smoke in both Germany and Russia." [3] And the basic principle of Soviet foreign trade policy was reasserted in an editorial which appeared in the same paper a few days later. "We must cease to make imports," it declared, "which, with better organization, can be produced at home. This does not in the least mean that we intend to cut down all our imports. We are for the expansion, not the restriction, of our ties with world economy; but at the same time we must strive to attain to a position where our foreign trade will contribute to our economic development, will contribute to the transformation of our country into an industrial country, a country producing machines. Our imports must serve to help us to assimilate up-to-date technical knowledge." [4]

[3] *Pravda,* April 28, 1930.
[4] *Pravda,* May 9, 1930.

Similar views were expressed by the official organ of the Soviet Government, the *Izvestia,* on the occasion of the signing of the Soviet-German trade agreement. "In politics," it said editorially, "love and affection are out of place. In politics one must be satisfied with mutual interests. The Soviet Union does not reproach the co-signatories of the agreement for the frankness of their declarations. On the contrary, we fully approve of realism in politics, and we can only express the wish that the industrialists of other countries will follow the lead of the German Chancellor, and, having satisfied themselves as to the strength of the Soviet Union and the risky nature of plans for intervention, may turn their attention to those business proposals and considerations to which the industrialization of the Union opens so broad a field. . . . There is no such thing on earth as absolute independence; and whatever our vast country may rise to, it will have this meaning alone, that we shall have sufficient strength to resist any attempt on the part of the capitalist world to reduce us to a state of slavery. It assuredly does not bar us from taking such advantage of the international division of labor as may be to our interest." [5] This interesting point of view was further developed by the *Izvestia* in a leading article which appeared two days later. "The Soviet Union is willing to develop its economic relations with the outside world, and to create the necessary conditions for their success. The growth of the economic strength of our

[5] *Izvestia,* April 21, 1931.

socialist country will be accompanied by the strengthening of its ties with the world market. It is impossible to prevent this process so long as there is *peaceful*[6] co-existence between the U. S. S. R. and its capitalist environment."[7] This point of view, which appears to us to be eminently sound, would seem, however, to be somewhat at variance with the oft-proclaimed intention of the Soviet to make the Union completely independent of the capitalist world. This independence, as the *Izvestia* pointed out, must be understood in a restricted sense.

FOREIGN RELATIONS

The desire for a *rapprochement* with other nations naturally found its expression in the foreign relations of the Soviet Union. Here, again, there was no sharp and definite break with earlier policies, but a gradual crystallization of the wish for a *modus vivendi*. The difficulties in this direction were numerous, and not all of them were of Soviet making. One of the severest blows suffered by the Soviet policies during this period was the breaking off of Anglo-Soviet relations in May, 1927. They were not resumed until October, 1929.

An impressive exhibition of the new attitude of the Soviet Union was given by the Soviet delegation to the World Economic Conference which met in Geneva in 1927. Here the official thesis of the

[6] Italics in the Russian text.
[7] *Izvestia,* April 23, 1931.

necessity of coöperation between the capitalist and the socialist system was solemnly proclaimed.

Even more spectacular, if perhaps somewhat tactless, was the program of disarmament outlined by M. Litvinov in Geneva, in November, 1927, at the League's Preparatory Commission on Disarmament. Litvinov demanded, it will be remembered, an "immediate, complete, and general disarmament" which was to be accomplished within a single year. Although of little practical value, this program served the purpose of announcing to the world Russia's freedom from aggressive intentions.

The seizure of the Chinese Eastern Railway by Chang Hsueh-liang on July 10, 1929, after the raid upon the Soviet consulate in Harbin, created an extremely tense international situation. The provocation was grave, and considerable alarm was felt throughout the world as to the immediate future of the Far East. The Briand-Kellogg Pact, to which the Soviet Government was a party, was invoked; but, after a certain exhibition of military force, the question was settled by direct negotiations between Moscow and Mukden; and the Chinese Eastern Railway returned to a régime of mixed Russo-Chinese management.

The Japanese occupation of Manchuria, which began in the middle of September, 1931, created a new situation that was fraught with danger. It must be said that on the whole, in the course of this painful development (which, at the time of writing,[8]

[8] March, 1933.

is still far from a definite settlement), the Soviet Government displayed a remarkable spirit of conciliation, one which it would be almost impossible to interpret in any way other than as proof that a desire to avoid war at any cost is the keynote of Soviet foreign policy. Of course, the Moscow foreign office and the Soviet press protested against the Japanese action, and movements of Soviet troops to the Manchurian frontier were often reported by the newspapers. Nevertheless, not only has the Soviet Union so far taken no action to prevent the Japanese occupation, but it has even—in February, 1932—granted Japan permission to use the Chinese Eastern Railway for the transportation of her troops, although this was an infringement of article 7 of the Portsmouth Treaty, as reaffirmed by the Soviet-Japanese convention of 1925, in which both parties agreed to use Manchurian railways exclusively for commercial purposes, and "in no wise for strategic purposes."

The events in Manchuria offered, among other things, an opportunity to Molotov, the President of the Council of People's Commissars, to voice the respect of his government for international treaties. "Our policy of non-interference in this Manchurian question," he declared, on November 6, 1931, "arises from our respect for the international treaties to which China is a party, from our respect for the sovereign rights and the independence of other nations, and from our unqualified rejection of any policy of military occupation and intervention. Whatever may be the formulæ and diplomatic gestures which attempt to disguise the policy of imperialistic intervention, the Soviet Union cannot but maintain to the very end a purely negative attitude toward such actions. No other attitude would be compatible with the policy adhered to by the U. S. S. R., or consistent with the defense by the Soviet Union of the interests of general peace." [9] We shall have further occasion to return to this assertion of the sanctity of international law, which is certainly most striking in the mouth of a communist leader. Indeed, there were probably doubts in the minds of the Moscow communists whether this newborn respect for international law might not be considered as treason to the cause of world proletarian revolution by their friends in the Far East. The *Izvestia* therefore took pains to explain that if the Red army was not with China, the heart of the Soviet Union was. "From the first days of the Far-Eastern conflict the U. S. S. R. has assumed a position of strict neutrality," it said. "It is, of course, unquestionable that the sympathy of the workers of the Soviet state is with the Chinese people, languishing as they do under the yoke of imperialistic exploiters. But this sympathy with the struggle of the Chinese workers and peasants in no way affects our attitude of rigid non-interference, which follows naturally upon the general peace policy of the Soviet Union." [10] The days of 1923, when the young communists burned with

[9] *Izvestia,* November 12, 1931.
[10] *Izvestia,* March 4, 1932.

the desire to rush from Moscow to Berlin, to fight for world revolution on the barricades of the German capital, were decidedly over. The Chinese workers and peasants had now to be satisfied with the sympathy of their Russian friends.

PACTS OF NON-AGGRESSION

Even more expressive, perhaps, than the Moscow government's attitude towards the Manchurian problem was the extraordinary enthusiasm which it developed for the so-called pacts of non-aggression. In this connection it may be interesting to recall the fact that the sixth congress of the Comintern discussed the question of aggression in war and made some comments which may be worth noting. In the case of a war between two bourgeois states, the congress decided, the problem does not even arise so long as the war is the inevitable product of imperialism. In the case of war between a bourgeois state and a revolutionary power the important question, again, is not which is the aggressor, but which is on the side of reaction, counter-revolution and exploitation, which is on the side of imperialism and against revolution.[11] These considerations do not seem to leave much room for a policy of pacts of non-aggression. Nevertheless the U. S. S. R. heartily embraced the idea even before it was receiving much attention in the world at large in connection with the Briand-Kellogg Pact. A number of non-aggression pacts were successfully negotiated by the Soviet

[11] Theses on the Struggle against Imperialist War, article 9.

Government with its Asiatic neighbors during the earlier years of its rule. This policy, which in Asia was perhaps not entirely inspired by the desire to promote peace, but also by that of strengthening Soviet influence among those Eastern peoples which were to play so important a part in world revolution, was extended in 1926 to European countries. Negotiations for the signing of a non-aggression pact with Poland were begun in August, 1926, but were interrupted by the murder of Voikov, the Soviet envoy to Poland, in June, 1927. Similar negotiations were opened with Latvia, Esthonia, and Finland, but without much success at the time. They were resumed at a later date, and resulted in the signing, in February, 1929, of the so-called Litvinov non-aggression protocol. The U.S.S.R., Esthonia, Latvia, Poland, and Rumania were parties to this agreement, and were later joined by Turkey and Persia. The U.S.S.R., in spite of the Litvinov protocol, insisted on negotiating direct non-aggression pacts with her immediate neighbors, this time with a considerable degree of success. In July, 1931, a non-aggression pact between the U.S.S.R. and Afghanistan was signed in Kabul. In the same year the existing non-aggression pacts between the U.S.S.R. and Lithuania, and the U.S.S.R. and Turkey, were renewed; and in September the U.S.S.R. and Italy entered into an agreement providing for an exchange of information with Russia on their respective armed forces. In January, 1932, the U.S.S.R. signed a non-aggression pact with Finland; in February, with Latvia; in May, with

Esthonia; in July, with Poland; in November, with France. This is a long and impressive list, at least for those who believe in non-aggression pacts, and the U. S. S. R. would seem to be among them. We may also add here that in December, 1932, the U. S. S. R. resumed diplomatic relations with China which had been broken off in 1927.

The importance attached by the U. S. S. R. to the non-aggression pacts may appear from the fact that, taking advantage of an interview with Mr. Kenkichi Yoshizawa, the newly appointed Japanese Minister of Foreign Affairs, who was in Moscow, on his way to Tokyo, in the last days of December, 1931,—this, too, at a time when the Manchurian crisis was in one of its most acute phases,—Litvinov, speaking for the Moscow Government, made the Japanese Minister the offer of a non-aggression pact. The negotiations lagged for months, and in January, 1933, Japan refused to sign it. Referring to the failure of the negotiations, Molotov is reported to have said at the meeting of the Executive Committee of the Soviets on January 23, 1933: "We hope Japan's refusal to sign is only temporary. Our position remains the same as before—one of neutrality and non-interference. But recently there have been false and unfriendly statements by certain Japanese officials, which do not better neighborly relations. Nevertheless, we shall continue our peaceful policy." [12] It is difficult to imagine how the spirit of concilia-

[12] Walter Duranty, in *New York Times*, January 24, 1933. The report of Molotov's speech which appeared in the *Pravda* of January 26, 1933, differs somewhat from that given by Mr. Duranty.

tion could go any farther. The keynote of the part
of Molotov's speech dealing with foreign relations
was the work that the U. S. S. R. had done for peace.

The Soviet Government takes the non-aggression
pacts very seriously, and they invariably enjoy an excellent press in the U. S. S. R. The following leading article published in the *Izvestia* on the occasion
of the ratification of the Russo-Polish Pact may
serve as a fair sample: "Soviet foreign policy was
never based on any 'orientation' except that of its
own strength, the growing attraction exercised upon
the masses by the policy of peace. We extended our
hand and offered a policy of peace to all countries;
and if some of them gave us a friendly answer more
speedily than others, it will suffice to speak of their
change of orientation. The Soviet Union has nothing
to change in its policy. We desire to live in peace
and collaboration, based on mutual advantages, with
all countries irrespective of their social and political
organization; and we are fighting only against those
who fight against us, who are preparing to make
war on us." [13] It is not unusual for the Soviet press
to sound a note of discreet caution. "No one can
suspect us of making a fetish of the significance of
these [non-aggression] pacts," the *Izvestia* remarked,
when discussing the proposed Soviet-Japanese pact;
"but there is no doubt that they are a certain ob-
stacle to preparation for war, a certain means for the
peaceful settlement of conflicts." [14]

[13] *Izvestia,* November 29, 1932.
[14] *Izvestia,* January 24, 1932.

The only non-aggression pact which invariably has a bad press in the U. S. S. R. is the Pact of Paris, or Briand-Kellogg Pact, which the Soviet Government signed in 1928. In doing so the Moscow government was careful to point out that it did not believe in the efficiency of the new international instrument and was signing it merely to avoid offering chances for any misrepresentations of its policy of peace. For Moscow claims, not only does the Briand-Kellogg Pact add nothing to the security of the world, but it is even harmful; for it is likely to breed illusions, and so obscure the real issues which the world proletariat has to face.[15] Some explanation of this attitude may be found, perhaps, in the vagueness of the provisions of the Pact of Paris and its all-comprehensive scope which, of course, cannot easily be reconciled with the communist conception of the development of the world. By communists, in fact, it is usually looked upon as just another attempt of the international bourgeoisie to encircle the U. S. S. R. But this, as we have seen, has not kept the Soviet Union from painstakingly building up its own system of non-aggression pacts, a system which is, perhaps, the most extensive in the world.

THE PROTOCOL FOR ECONOMIC NON-AGGRESSION

Moscow's peace effort, it will be remembered, is only one of two pillars of Soviet foreign policy, and, in a sense, it is merely a corollary of the second

---

[15] See, for instance, *Pakt Kellogga (The Kellogg Pact)* in *Kommunisticheski Internatsional,* No. 35 (161), 1928, pp. 8–11.

and more important pillar, economic coöperation with the capitalist nations. Both are necessary conditions for the success of the industrialization of the U. S. S. R.; a war or obstacles to the normal development of Soviet foreign trade will inevitably retard the fulfillment of the Five Year Plan and its successor and may well be fatal to it. The discrimination against Soviet exports by a number of nations and the threats of even worse reprisals often voiced in the foreign press and in foreign parliaments, when something brings up the subject of Soviet dumping, have led the Soviet Government to lay before the Commission of Inquiry for European Union an interesting document known as the Protocol for Economic Non-aggression. The idea, no doubt, was inspired by the success of the Soviet non-aggression pacts which we have discussed. The general lines of Soviet policy were admirably stated at Geneva on May 18, 1931, by M. Litvinov, who appeared as the chief Soviet delegate. What he had to say was remarkable, not only by reason of its contents, but also because of its form, which was sober and businesslike, and displayed a complete absence of those offensive and provocative remarks in which he was wont to indulge in the past.

"While pointing to the influence for good which the Soviet Union's foreign trade had in the present world crisis," he said, "I am far from desirous of creating the impression that there is a harmony of interest between the two systems—the capitalistic and the Soviet—now existing in Europe. The dif-

ficulties between these two systems exist and will
continue to exist. These two systems are struggling
and will continue to struggle against each other from
the very nature of their existence and development.
The question is whether this struggle and development will be allowed to follow a natural process or
whether both systems will have recourse from day
to day to mutual hostile measures which can have
no decisive influence on the outcome of the struggle,
but will turn out to be two-edged weapons. . . . It
would be naïve to expect capitalist states consciously
and impartially to assist in the setting up of socialism in the Soviet Union, or the latter consciously
to further the strengthening of the capitalist system.
The question can only be one of economic agreements in dealing between the capitalist countries and
the Soviet Union, mutually advantageous for all
parties concerned, and for which there is ample
scope. I am leaving aside for the moment the possibility of military attack on the Soviet Union and
have in view a peaceful period of given duration." [16]

The preamble of the draft protocol offered by
Litvinov may be worth quoting in full. It is as follows: "The representatives of the undersigned countries recognize that: (a) The mitigation of the crisis
which has overtaken the national economy of most
countries requires, in addition to abstention from
war as a measure for the solution of international
conflicts, the complete cessation of all forms of eco-

[16] League of Nations, *Commission of Inquiry for European
Union*, Geneva, 1931, p. 34.

nomic aggression, both avowed and concealed, by any country or groups of countries, against any other countries or groups of countries; (b) The cessation of economic aggression is an essential condition for the peaceful coöperation of states in the sphere of economics, irrespective of their political-economic systems; (c) The cessation of economic aggression would help to put an end to the present atmosphere of distrust, uncertainty, and alarm, weighing so heavily upon the economic position."

Whatever one may think of the practical value of the draft protocol suggested by Litvinov, it will readily be admitted that it gives concise expression to the policy which the Soviet Government has worked out in the course of recent years. The brief outline of the policy of Moscow which we have presented supplies sufficient evidence that it was a great deal more than an empty diplomatic gesture. The history of the protocol since May, 1931, is not particularly encouraging. It was referred to a subcommittee and no action on it has been taken so far. Litvinov made several efforts to bring about a decision, but without success. The question was again discussed in Geneva in October, 1932.[17]

PROBLEMS OF RECONSTRUCTION

An eloquent proof of the new attitude of the Soviet Government is the dwindling interest in foreign problems, except in the case of the prevention of imperialistic wars, as evidenced by the

[17] *Izvestia,* October 3, 1932.

press, public utterances of Soviet leaders, and the resolutions of various Soviet and communist bodies. Since the fourteenth congress of the Russian Communist Party in 1925 sanctioned the policy of socialist industrialization which eventually took the shape of the first and second Five Year Plans, the attention of the nation has centred itself more and more upon economic problems. While reports on the international situation and the progress of the world revolutionary movement were still included in the agendas of the various official gatherings, they took on the character of mere matters of ritual or protocol observances which one went through rather as a matter of form before entering upon the discussion of questions which really mattered, such as the building of new factories, the organization of supplies, the collectivization of farming, and the planning of the great socialist state of the future. So far as the development of communist theory is concerned, practically nothing has been done since the sixth congress of the Comintern in 1928, and the communist leaders of Russia, absorbed in their far-stretching plans, have been content to repeat with a rather wearying monotony those revolutionary formulæ with which we are already familiar.

There is, no doubt, a flagrant contradiction between that policy of peace which, we believe, the Soviet Union has sincerely at heart, and what, according to official proclamation, the "third period" is to be. For it will be remembered, this period, that of the present, is to be a period of growing antagonisms within the capitalist system, antagonisms leading to inevitable wars among the imperialistic nations, wars against the U. S. S. R., and gigantic class struggles. This "third period" is still a part of the official communist dogma, a rather uncomfortable one considering that the imperialist wars have so far failed to materialize (except, perhaps, in Manchuria) and considering that the U. S. S. R. is earnestly determined to do everything in its power to prevent them. The question naturally arises, why do these imperialistic and "inevitable" wars so long delay their coming? The answer to this question was suggested by Stalin as far back as 1926, when he advanced the proposition that the proletariat of the capitalist nations, although not yet sufficiently strong to overthrow the exploiters at home, was nevertheless strong enough to prevent them from launching attacks against the U. S. S. R.[18] This argument was reiterated by Stalin in a picturesque form at the sixteenth congress of the Russian Communist Party in June–July, 1930. "Intervention is a weapon that is sharp at both ends," he said. "Of this the capitalists are fully aware. It is all right, they think, if intervention will work out smoothly and will end in the defeat of the U. S. S. R. But what are they to do if it ends in the defeat of the capitalists? . . . And what about the workers in the capitalist countries who will block such inter-

[18] *Puti Mirovoi Revolyutsii (The Ways of the World Revolution)*, verbatim report of the seventh plenary session of the Executive Committee of the Communist International, Moscow—Leningrad, 1927, Vol. II, p. 12.

vention in the affairs of the U. S. S. R., who will fight against intervention, and who, if necessary, may strike at the capitalists from the rear? . . . This explains the trend that makes for the continuation of peaceful relations with the U. S. S. R." [19] And the congress accordingly passed a resolution which declared that "the growing economic strength of the U. S. S. R., increasing the danger and risk of bourgeois intervention in the U. S. S. R., especially under the conditions of the present crisis and the ever-growing revolutionary movement, forces certain groups of the bourgeoisie to seek the development and consolidation of economic ties with the U. S. S. R." [20] It was also at this congress that Stalin uttered the celebrated statement which has since been repeated in hundreds of articles, speeches, resolutions, and army orders: "We do not want a single bit of foreign land. But at the same time, not an inch of our land shall ever yield to anyone else." [21] Assuredly, too, this sounds rather more like the utterance of some fine, old-style emperor or king than one from the leader of the world proletarian revolution.

The relatively rare references of the Soviet leaders to international affairs, when they do not indulge in the repetition of the somewhat faded formulæ of the sixth congress of the Comintern, deal invariably

[19] *Shestnadtsati Sezd Vsesoyuznoi Kommunisticheskoi Partii Bolshevikov (Sixteenth Congress of the Communist Party of the Soviet Union)*, verbatim report, June 26–July 13, 1930, Moscow—Leningrad, 1930, p. 23.

[20] *Ibid.*, p. 712.

[21] *Ibid.*, p. 24.

with the necessity of closer economic collaboration with the outside world. Even the head of the Red army, Voroshilov, in a speech delivered in May, 1930, devoted much of his time to this subject. Naturally, he did not omit the usual references to the inevitability of a war between socialism and capitalism, and he paid conventional compliments to the Red army. But his military utterances were clearly subordinated to the recognition of the advantages Russia was deriving from its peaceful intercourse with other countries.[22] When, in an address delivered in June, 1930, Kalinin, the president —after a fashion—of the Soviet Union, had enumerated the factors that indicated the growth of Russia's foreign trade, he declared that it was "of immense significance, both politically and economically, to the parties involved, because it opened broad possibilities for the development of business coöperation and the consolidation of peace in Europe." [23]

Most instructive was the speech delivered by Molotov in March, 1931. At the end of his survey of the progress made in Soviet foreign trade and of the place occupied by the Soviet Union in the world market (he regretted that it had yet to equal Russia's pre-war level), Molotov declared that the development of foreign economic relations of the Union was to the mutual benefit of all parties concerned. "The interests of our socialist upbuilding

[22] *Izvestia,* June 17, 1930. Similar views were expressed by Voroshilov on other occasions, for instance, in his address delivered at the celebrations of May 1, 1932.

[23] *Izvestia,* June 19, 1930.

are inseparably bound up with the development of peaceful relations with other countries, and the progress of economic intercourse between the U. S. S. R. and these countries." This aim, the aim of strengthening peaceful relations and forming economic ties with other nations, has invariably been the foundation of the policy of the Soviet Government during the period now under review. But even more significant, perhaps, were the closing words of Molotov's address. "At the Economic Conference of 1927," he said, "our delegates made the following statement: 'Socialism is not merely a system of economic and social equality. Socialism, first of all, means peace. The contradictions between the two economic systems, which during a certain historical period, must unavoidably co-exist, do not exclude the possibility of some practical arrangement between them.' To-day we still hold the same view. We also believe that, as a matter of policy, this attitude of the Soviet Government is justified by the course of events. When we speak of the necessary co-existence during a certain historical period of two social systems which are based on contradictory principles—capitalism and socialism—we draw therefrom *our* particular inferences. We are aware that the bourgeoisie likewise draws therefrom inferences peculiar to *it* alone. Our inferences are that the said historical period must be used to the utmost to gain the victory for our system. The purpose of our enemy is to annihilate the Soviet state, the socialist state. Two worlds are brought face to face.

A struggle is going on between these two worlds. Our purpose is the establishment of socialism in the U. S. S. R. and the carrying on of the world struggle for the cause of communism, for the complete victory of the cause of Marx-Engels-Lenin." [24] This declaration met with thunders of applause.

In his remarks before moving the adjournment of the sixth congress of the Soviets, on March 13, 1931, Molotov reiterated the basic principles of the Soviet policy. "Our fundamental task," he said, "is to fulfil the Five Year Plan and to assure the further success of socialist construction. This determines the home policies of the Soviet Government and our foreign policy as well. Our watchword remains unaltered—a struggle for the maintenance of international peace, and the strengthening of peaceful relations with other countries." [25]

It would be easy, but useless, to multiply these quotations. Molotov's address in January, 1933, to which we have referred in the earlier part of this chapter, does not differ in general tenure from what he said twenty months before. From the beginning of the period of industrialization, the foreign policy of the Soviet Union has been completely overshadowed by the requirements of the Five Year Plan, which practically controls it.

ANOTHER FORWARD STEP

According to the German adage, he who has said A must also say B. The parting of the ways be-

[24] *Izvestia*, March 11 and 12, 1931.
[25] *Izvestia*, March 14, 1931.

tween the U. S. S. R. and world revolution began with the adoption of "socialism in a single country," and gradually led the Soviet Union to a policy of fairly close and, we may say, friendly, coöperation with its class enemies. That the Moscow government is not unwilling to face the logical consequences of its earlier decisions has been demonstrated by the statements made by M. Litvinov at Geneva on February 6, 1933. Addressing the Disarmament Conference, he suggested that the signatories of the Pact of Paris should drop their reservations thereto, and he submitted his own definition of an aggressor. Without mentioning Japan by name, Litvinov went into the various arguments advanced by her in defense of her Manchurian policy and rejected them one by one. It was clear that in accordance with Litvinov's views Japan was guilty of breaches of international agreements on a dozen counts.[26] The Geneva audience was thus confronted with the piquant picture of the Soviet delegate upholding the sanctity of international commitments against Japan, that torch-bearer of western civilization in the Far East.

It will be remembered that the Soviets' entry into the lists as the champions of international law was not really a new thing, and that similar ideas were advanced, for instance, by Molotov in November, 1931. What is interesting about M. Litvinov's Geneva speech is the vast importance attached to it in Moscow. The *Izvestia* described it editorially on February 8, 1933, as "the people's charter of rights

[26] *New York Times,* February 7, 1933.

to security and independence." After reiterating the Soviet desire for that security which would open the way to a reduction of armaments—that is, the acceptance of the French thesis that security must come first and disarmament later—the *Izvestia* laid down a policy which could not fail to meet with a friendly reception in Germany. The Soviet declaration, it said, did not mean the final acceptance of existing frontiers, for they did not always represent national interests. But the changes desired must be brought about by agreement, not by war. Particularly important in connection with our study is the following statement of the Soviet official organ: "Litvinov's declaration not only is aimed against intervention in a country where there is a revolution, but in the name of the U. S. S. R. undertakes the obligation not to intervene in a country where there is a counter-revolution." Commenting on this significant declaration, Mr. Walter Duranty remarks that M. Litvinov has promised on behalf of the Soviet Union that it "will take no aggressive action should Germany, Poland, or Rumania be faced by a revolutionary movement. No other interpretation of the *Izvestia's* comment is possible." [27] We are fully in agreement with Mr. Duranty's inferences. But what an extraordinary attitude for the knights-errant of world revolution, and how is it to be brought in line with the commitments of the Russian Communist Party which controls the government, commitments to do everything in its power

[27] *New York Times,* February 9, 1933.

to foster the great social upheaval? Not even a Soviet government can at one and the same time destroy capitalism and collaborate with it. Moscow was faced with the necessity of making its choice. What the choice was has been clearly indicated in the comments of the *Izvestia* on Litvinov's speech at Geneva.

THE THIRD INTERNATIONAL

But if Moscow has, in practice, virtually abandoned its international revolutionary activities, and is even willing to say so officially, the question at once arises, what is the position of the Third International, the great general staff of world revolution? The answer is given in our analysis of the Program of the Comintern, and it is an answer that would seem to indicate that the Comintern has gradually been transformed into an international body whose chief and immediate goal is the defense of the Soviet Union, in spite of the transparent veil of revolutionary phraseology inherited from Marx, Engels, and Lenin. The truth of the matter seems to be that the Third International has suffered a complete eclipse. We have already pointed out that international affairs have been pushed into the background of the Soviet press and public discussion. The Comintern has suffered a similar fate and, indeed, references to its activities are rarely to be found in the Soviet newspapers or in the resolutions of the Soviet bodies. No congress of the Comintern has been called since 1928. Its permanent organization, no doubt, continues to exist and to perform its routine duties, but Trotsky was probably right when he said that it is now merely another government department, in the work of which few but its own employees take any interest. The members of the Russian Communist Party, we may infer, have been persuaded not to take too much interest in the international labor movement; and newspaper information bearing upon international labor questions, it is suggested, is to-day not what it used to be before the war.[28] The days when disquisitions upon the approaching world revolution occupied most of the space in Soviet journals are a thing of the past. In recent years the Third International has been not unlike one of these numerous international organizations which, since the war, have sprung up all over the world, growths that have, above all, multiplied on the shores of the Lake of Geneva. They may be described as organizations which lead an uneventful and obscure existence and whose functions, like their very names, usually disguised under some undecipherable and often strange combination of letters, are a standing mystery to a vast majority of a public otherwise fairly well-informed.

But if the activities of the Third International have been bereft of much of their former lustre, they have neverthless continued. The Executive Committee of the Comintern meets at more or less regular

[28] Léon Trotsky, *L'internationale communiste après Lénine*, p. 397.

intervals, and solemnly discusses the progress of world revolution as if no change had taken place in the general orientation of the citadel of world communism, Red Moscow. There, the twelfth plenary session of the Executive Committee was held in the autumn of 1932, and the results of its deliberations were given to the world under conditions which are in themselves highly significant. The "Theses and Resolutions" adopted by the twelve sessions did not appear at all in the *Izvestia*, that official organ of the Soviet Government. They were given a conspicuous position in the *Pravda* of October 11, 1932, but, oddly enough, in the form of a reprint from *L'Humanité*, the organ of the French Communist Party. This, presumably, was the method chosen in Moscow to emphasize the frail barrier which separates the Soviet Government from the Communist International, the *Pravda* being, as we know, the mouthpiece of the Russian Communist Party. Why, however, the decisions of the Executive Committee were not communicated directly to the *Pravda* but had to reach it via its French contemporary, is something we are at a loss to explain.

On this occasion the *Pravda* published an appropriate leading article in which, in accordance with unfailing communist tradition, it described the "Theses and Resolutions" as being "immensely significant to the international revolutionary movement." The quality of these outgivings, however, hardly justifies the use of superlatives. They follow closely the pattern which has invariably been used since the sixth congress of the Comintern. In our desire to present a comprehensive record of the policy of the Comintern and of the U.S.S.R., we shall briefly summarize them at the risk of being tedious, and repeating what we have said before. The "Thesis on the End of Capitalist Stabilization and the Growth of the U.S.S.R." reiterates the familiar theory of the rapid progress in the disintegration of capitalism, and of the important part played in it by the economic reconstruction of the Soviet Union. The crisis in the capitalist world is entering upon a phase particularly acute; the revolutionary movement is growing; antagonisms between capitalist nations are also growing, and they manifest themselves in measures of economic war and the race for armaments; hurried preparations are being made for the organization of bourgeois intervention against the U.S.S.R. The further concentration of financial capital and the decline in the sum-total of profits accentuate the struggle for markets, and conflicts between capital and labor. All these conditions inevitably lead to wars between nations and between classes. The "Thesis on the New World War" deals with the approaching armed conflict which has already begun in the Far East and which directly affects the United States, Japan, and Great Britain. "Only the firm peace policy of the U.S.S.R., the fear of the bourgeoisie that the imperialistic war will be transformed into civil war, and apprehensions of colonial uprisings have so far prevented capitalism from using the weapon of war and intervention."

The "Thesis on the Dictatorship of the Bourgeoisie, Nationalism, Fascism, and Social-Fascism" denounces those reactionary tendencies of the bourgeois governments which, in themselves, indicate the growing weakness of such governments. The economic crisis has stimulated the growth of extreme nationalism. Fascism and Social-Fascism are merely the servants of capital. The social-democratic leaders, with their program of state control of the various branches of industry, are merely traitors to the cause of the working classes. Their influence is distinctly on the wane. The "Thesis on the Upward Revolutionary Trend and the Preparation for the Struggle for the Dictatorship of the Proletariat" enumerates the revolutionary developments in different parts of the world: China, Spain, Poland, Germany, Great Britain, Czechoslovakia, France, Belgium, India, Japan, and the United States, where for example, there are cited the current strikes, and the demonstrations of veterans, farmers, and the unemployed. In the course of the last sixteen years the communist movement has grown in strength in many countries, for instance, in Germany, China, Poland, Czechoslovakia, Spain, and Finland. "In spite of the weakness of the influence of the communist parties upon the masses in a number of countries," the Thesis declares, "in the whole capitalist world the communists have proven themselves, in numerous battles and trials, to be a gallant and truly revolutionary vanguard of the proletariat." The time still to elapse before the outbreak of the revo-

lutionary crisis is running short, and it is imperative
to use it to the full for the "bolshevization" of the
masses. In order to achieve this purpose, it is the
duty of the national communist parties to maintain
close and active ties with the workers at large, with
communist and non-communist organizations of
labor, with the trade unions, and with the unemployed. The communist parties must devise comprehensive and popular slogans, they must build up
the "united front of labor" from below, and they
must strengthen their own party organization. They
must be ready for any emergency. The "Thesis on
the Immediate Aims of the National Communist
Parties" lays down the following familiar rules:
Struggle against the advance of capital! Struggle
against Fascism and reaction! Struggle against imperialistic wars and intervention against the
U.S.S.R.! The best method for achieving these
goals is the preparation of mass political strikes as
one of the immediate links in the chain of proletarian
struggle. The Thesis then examines the more concrete policies which are to be followed by the communist parties in each country.

This brief summary may suffice, we hope, to indicate that the twelfth plenary session of the Executive Committee of the Comintern added nothing
to what had been said on many previous occasions
by its predecessors. That the *Pravda* found it necessary to describe its decisions as "immensely significant to the international revolutionary movement"
is in itself a telling comment on that debility from

which, we believe, the Third International is suffering. Those who choose to base their opinion of the foreign policies pursued by the U. S. S. R. on the dead letter of communist doctrine will find in the Theses of the twelfth session plenty of ammunition to support their views. Such pronouncements are hardly compatible with the policy of coöperation which has been repeatedly supported by the Soviet Government in both Moscow and Geneva. We have no desire to minimize the discrepancy. But we feel that here, as on many other occasions, words are not deeds. And in the light of our earlier examination of the matter, the twelfth session of the Executive Committee notwithstanding, we fully agree with the "strange paradox" which has been shrewdly noted by one of America's most competent students of the Soviet Union, Mr. Walter Duranty; namely, "that the Bolshevist Kremlin to-day regards the growth of the revolutionary movement in Europe with real anxiety." [29]

SOCIALISM VS. CAPITALISM

To those who have been patient enough to follow us in this discussion, "the strange paradox" may appear not quite so strange, although it undoubtedly remains a paradox. Since the beginning of the present economic depression, in the Soviet Union it has become customary to contrast the economic progress of the U. S. S. R. with the decline of capitalism. As the *Izvestia* puts it, "The Soviet Union is the only

[29] *New York Times*, November 20, 1932.

country immune from the economic crisis which is playing havoc in the capitalist world." [30] It is confidently expected that at the end of the second Five Year Plan the U. S. S. R. will occupy the first place in Europe from the point of view of industrial development and will no longer be dependent on the older industrial nations for importations of machinery and industrial equipment. "The success of socialism in the U. S. S. R. is the best proof of the advantages of the socialist system as opposed to that of capitalism," declared a resolution of the seventeenth conference of the Russian Communist Party. "In the capitalist states we find severe unemployment among millions of industrial workers and terrible impoverishment of the multimillion masses of the rural populations. In the Soviet Union we have a complete liquidation of unemployment, the elimination of pauperism, the seven-hour day in factories and workshops, and a steady improvement in the welfare of the working classes in both cities and rural communities." [31] That this picture is far too rosy is plain to anyone who has followed economic developments in the Soviet Union. And that economic independence of the outside world which the government of Moscow has so much at heart is still a thing of the future, if it can be achieved at all. As we have seen, the necessity of international economic col-

---

[30] *Izvestia*, September 5, 1931.

[31] *Semnadtsataya Konferentsya Vsesoyuznoi Kommunisticheskoi Partii Bolshevikov (Seventeenth Conference of the Communist Party of the Soviet Union)*, January 30–February 4, 1932, verbatim report, Moscow, 1932, p. 280.

laboration at the present time has been emphasized over and over again by the Soviet leaders. The Five Year Plan and the "control figures" on which the whole scheme of industrialization is based have for their point of departure the volume of Soviet exports; and they, for their part, determine the volume of much needed imports. It is only too obvious that the volume of exports depends on the buying capacity of the world market and the unhampered flow of international trade. Grandiloquent declarations which point to the immunity of the U. S. S. R. from the effects of the world depression are hardly more than empty gestures and propaganda. The plain truth of the situation is that under existing conditions prosperity in one country, whether socialist or capitalist, is a mere illusion, as the wealthiest nations of the world begin to learn from the bitter experiences of the last few years. In theory, of course, it is possible to imagine that a large country with a numerous population and possessing necessary natural resources, can establish a self-contained national economy that is entirely independent of the rest of the world, just as it is possible, again in theory, for an individual to return to the hunting and fishing stage, and to supply himself with the bare necessaries of life without outside help. In both cases, however, this self-sufficiency can be achieved only at the price of most exorbitant sacrifices, the lowering of all accepted standards of living, and the renunciation of that elusive and indefinite thing which we call modern civilization. For good or evil the nations of the world have grown and progressed together, and the sooner this fact receives that recognition which is long overdue, the brighter will be the prospects for a better future.

It seems reasonable to assume that the Soviet leaders, whatever may be their plans for the distant future, are under no such illusions in the present. Mr. Duranty again speaks truly when he writes that "Moscow is now watching Europe with a keen premonition of disaster it feels almost powerless to avert. Far from trying to foment revolution, the U.S.S.R. to-day is ready and eager to coöperate in any sincere attempt to combat the effects of the depression and to restore the economic order." [32] It is precisely to this conclusion that we have been led by our whole analysis. [32]

THE DILEMMA

If we attempt to take a bird's-eye view of the entire course of Soviet foreign relations from 1917 to the beginning of 1933, and also of the leading ideas

[32] *New York Times*, November 22, 1932.

[33] The sensational trial of six British engineers and thirty-five Russians on charges of espionage, bribery, and sabotage took place at a time when the manuscript of this book was already in the hands of the publishers. It will be remembered that the six Britishers, all of them officers of the Metropolitan-Vickers Company, a British firm dealing in electrical machinery and turbines and operating in the Soviet Union for about ten years, were arrested in Moscow by the Soviet political police on March 11 and 12. Two of them, Allan Monkhouse and Charles Nordwall, were released on March 14; and three more—William H. Thornton, John Cushny, and A. L. Gregory—were released on bail on April 4. William L. MacDonald was the only accused Britisher who remained in prison throughout the trial. The trial lasted from April 12 to April 19. Gregory was acquitted. Monkhouse,

which underlie it, we are confronted with a curious situation. We see the gradual, painful, but unmistakable transformation of a group of professional revolutionaries who, by an extraordinary concurrence of economic, social, and political factors found themselves at the head of a vast empire. They began by being the knights-errant of world revolution and they have become the artisans of the vast, if somewhat prosaic, tasks of constructing from the raw material of a desperately poor and backward nation the great industrialized socialist common-

Nordwall, and Cushny were deported from Russia for five years. Thornton was sentenced to three years in prison, and MacDonald —two years. Both Thornton and MacDonald made signed confessions. Thornton, however, repudiated his confession during the trial on the ground that it was made under "moral pressure" while MacDonald maintained his plea of guilty to the very end.

It would be hardly wise to venture at the present stage any definite opinion on the nature of this remarkable trial and the real motive behind it. The confessions of Thornton and MacDonald are among the most puzzling features unless one is prepared to accept the guilt of the British engineers. It must be remembered, on the other hand, that "confessions" in Soviet sabotage trials occur with the most amazing regularity and on a scale entirely without parallel in the courts of the capitalist countries. The extraordinary leniency shown by the court to the British defendants stands in sharp contrast with the usual stern severity of Soviet justice. Five of the six defendants accused of a crime punishable by death were permitted to remain at liberty before and during the trial, a case probably without precedent in the annals of any court. The verdict, too, was remarkably mild, carrying one acquittal, three purely nominal sentences of deportation, and only two prison sentences, both of them surprisingly short if one takes into consideration the gravity of the charges. It has also been reported in the American press that the two imprisoned British engineers are enjoying particularly favored treatment and most unusual privileges. All this seems to indicate that, whatever might have been the origins of the trial, the Soviet Government has not abandoned that policy of coöperation with the capitalist countries which it has been consistently building up in the course of the last few years. At the time of the present writing (May 10, 1933) the pleas of Thornton and MacDonald for a commutation of their sentences are

wealth of the future. The turning point in this process of transformation is the adoption of Stalin's doctrine of socialism in a single country. These builders of factories and plants, these matter-of-fact leaders in the colossal project of large-scale collective farms, these communist tribunes who have banned religion as a vulgar superstition, owe allegiance to the revolutionary doctrines of Marx, Engels, and Lenin. Their doctrines have been revised and readjusted in order to meet the requirements of a new order of things, but there is still a wide, and, it would

still pending and may prove a way out of the impasse in the Anglo-Soviet relations. See *below,* p. 253.

Immediately after the verdict became known in London, the British Government imposed an embargo on a number of articles imported from the Soviet Union amounting to something like 80 per cent of Great Britain's imports from the U. S. S. R. The Soviet Government retaliated three days later by an embargo on British goods and by a prohibition of chartering British vessels. On this occasion Maxim Litvinov, Soviet Commissar for Foreign Affairs, issued the following interesting statement dealing with the principles on which the commercial relations of the Soviet Union with foreign countries are conducted: "Russian external trade policy is based on firm foundations which have not been altered since the beginning of our foreign trade, and which we do not propose to alter in the future. This policy is based on: (1) Economic intercourse between countries of the world, and particularly between major powers irrespective of social and political systems obtaining in them. (2) Advantages accruing to each country from trade with other countries and confidence between the contracting countries based on a real solvency approved by the fulfillment of commercial and financial obligations. (3) Absence of political upheavals in relations between trading countries as an inherent condition of stability of trade relations. (4) Liberty for official representatives of trading countries to fulfill the normal functions necessary for trade. (5) Lawful intercourse between governmental representatives and citizens of trading countries. (6) Subjection of foreigners to the jurisdiction of countries where they are resident. Elasticity of imports is an exclusive peculiarity of the Soviet Union. Regarding the elasticity of our imports, it should be borne in mind that not only their very wide expansion, but also their contraction is possible." (*New York Times,* April 23, 1933).

appear, an unbridgeable gap between the practical politics of the U. S. S. R. and the teachings of communism. The U. S. S. R. has never repudiated, and so long as it remains communist cannot repudiate, the doctrine of world revolution which is inscribed in letters of fire on its banner. The peaceful evolution from capitalism to communism—and it still remains to be proved that capitalism is doomed—is ruled out; the change is one that must be brought about by violent methods, through the class struggle and the dictatorship of the proletariat.

Any intelligent student of the Russian situation who desires to grasp the real significance of the U. S. S. R. as a factor in international politics is confronted with a dilemma. On one hand, there is an unquestionably earnest, sustained and determined effort to raise the masses of the Russian people from that state of ignorance, poverty, misery, and unhappiness which has been their fate in the past, and make of them thinking and intelligent human beings. The method by which this is to be achieved may appear to us unsound, objectionable, and even criminal. We may think, and perhaps with good ground, that the effort is certain to fail. But the purpose itself—the abolition of the exploitation of man by man, and the creation of a human society which will reduce to a minimum the misery and sufferings which we see everywhere in the capitalist world of to-day—this purpose cannot but commend itself to a great many people who are averse to the communist doctrines. It is towards the promotion of this purpose that the policy of the U. S. S. R. has been directed, during the past decade, a policy carried on by methods which, to repeat, we have no desire to defend.

On the other hand, we find a body of scholastic doctrines which are couched in the uncompromising terms of class struggle, the "inevitable" downfall of capitalism, imperialistic wars, civil wars, colonial uprisings, and the dictatorship of the proletariat—all the harsh and terrible vocabulary of the revolutionary teachings of Marx, Engels, and Lenin. On the one side we have the insistent bids for a closer cooperation with the world at large and promises of non-aggression; on the other, the pledges to support world revolution by all the means at the disposal of the U. S. S. R. (in spite of Litvinov's offer at Geneva) and the fomenting of that revolutionary unrest which is, it is true, to lead the remainder of the world to a millennium, but only by the long and painful road of the proletarian dictatorship, and at the price of the destruction of all that we have grown to love and cherish.

Which of the two speaks for the real Russia of to-day? And who must truly represent her? Is it the bearded and black-frocked German professor and his disciple, Lenin, with their elaborate and dubious schemes of world revolution, their "general" and "immediate" revolutionary situations, their "inevitable downfall of capitalism"? Or is it the young workmen and peasants, awkwardly approaching beautiful new machines and tractors which they have never even dreamed of before, or standing dazzled by the wonders of the future as unfolded by their leaders, who promise to lay the entire world at their feet? Is it the young men and women who see at last a way of escape from the bleak drudgery of the old Russian village and are eager to conquer the world —though not necessarily by the use of arms?

POSTSCRIPT

Two events bearing immediately on the questions discussed in this book have taken place in the early days of July, too late to be included in the body of the text. I feel nevertheless that they must be brought to the attention of the reader.

The first of them is the signature in London on July 1, 1933, of a non-aggression pact between the U. S. S. R., Poland, Rumania, Turkey, Esthonia, Latvia and Finland,[1] a further step in that policy of cooperation which I have discussed in my last chapter.

The second is the successful termination of the negotiations between Sir John Simon and M. Litvinov dealing with the case of the two engineers of the Metropolitan-Vickers Company serving their sentences in a Russian prison. On July 1, 1933, the London Foreign Office issued the following statement:

"The Soviet Embassy have informed the Secre-

[1] *Le Temps*, July 3, 1933.

tary of State for Foreign Affairs that the petitions of Messrs. Thornton and MacDonald, who were sentenced in April last to terms of imprisonment of three years and two years respectively, came before the Praesidium of the Executive Committee of the Soviets to-day (Saturday) and that the sentences have been commuted, so that both men are to leave Soviet territory immediately. They are being liberated this evening. At the same time the Commissar for Trade has cancelled the counter-embargo against British imports.

"A supplement to the *London Gazette* published this evening contains a proclamation made by the King in Council to-day revoking the embargo which was declared by the previous Proclamation of April 19 made under Section 1 of the Russian Goods (Import Prohibition) Act, 1933.

"Arrangements will now promptly be made to resume Anglo-Soviet trade negotiations at the point where they were interrupted in consequence of the arrest of the Metropolitan-Vichers engineers." [2]

This happy solution of the unfortunate incident of March 11 closely follows the lines I ventured to suggest in an earlier page.

Both these developments would seem to corroborate the conclusions of my last chapter.

July 4, 1933,
   Paris.

[2] *The Times* (London), July 3, 1933.

INDEX

A

Afghanistan, non-aggression pact with, 224.

Africa, 188.

Allied Powers, shocked by Russia ending war, 34; backing White movement, 34–35, 75; policy revised, 74. *See also* Blockade, White movement.

Allies, Supreme Council of, 74.

Alma Ata, Trotsky deported to, 128.

America, Engels on revolution in, 133; in imperialistic struggle, 137. *See also* United States.

Amtorg, 64.

Anarchism, 192.

Anarchists, 103.

Anarchy of production, 129, 170, 180.

Anglo-Russian Committee, 212–214.

Archangel, evacuated, 74.

Argentina, 188.

Armistice of November 11, 1918, 34, 38, 74.

Army, Red. *See* Red Army.

Austria, revolutionary situation in, 36; Zinoviev on prospect of revolution in, 77; preserves bourgeois government, 78; progress of revolution watched, 111.

Austria-Hungary, propaganda in, 35.

Austro-Marxism, 192.

B

Balkans, Zinoviev on prospect of revolution in, 77; failure of revolution in, 78; alleged semi-feudal conditions in, 188.

Bela Kun, collapse of his rule, 75. *See also* Hungary.

Belgium, revolutionary development in, 243.

"Bloc," formed by Trotsky and the Opposition, 127–128, 159–160.

Blockade of Russia, 35, 62; abandoned, 74, 170–171.

Bolsheviks. *See* Social Democratic Party, Russian.

"Bolshevization," 117, 244.

Borodin, Michael, activities in China, 173–174.

Brazil, 188.

Brest-Litovsk, Treaty of, 17, 34, 35, 38, 111, 126.

Briand-Kellogg Pact, 65, 220, 223, 227, 237.

Bukharin, Nicholas, Lenin on, 12, 201; on Brest-Litovsk negotiations, 37; on revolutionary outlook in 1919, 44–45; at third congress of Comintern, 96; political future uncertain, 107; on New Economic Policy, 114–115; early view of socialism in a single country, 152; on significance of Russian revolution, 163–164; at sixth congress of Comintern, 175, 176, 178, 196; on "third